Xmas 14

Dad from Dan

COLLISON

THE PACIFIC SHORE

COLOR PHOTOGRAPHS BY
DENNIS BROKAW
HUMAN AND NATURAL HISTORY BY
AND WESLEY MARX

———————

THE PACIFIC SHORE
MEETING PLACE OF
MAN AND NATURE

E. P. DUTTON & CO., INC. | NEW YORK | 1974

Grateful acknowledgment is made for permission to quote from the following sources:

"The Purse-Seine," *The Selected Poetry of Robinson Jeffers.* Copyright 1937 by Robinson Jeffers. Copyright © 1965 by Donnan Jeffers and Garth Jeffers. Reprinted by permission of Random House, Inc.

"A Redeemer," *The Selected Poetry of Robinson Jeffers.* Copyright 1928 by Robinson Jeffers, renewed © 1956 by Robinson Jeffers. Reprinted by permission of Random House, Inc.

"Return," *The Selected Poetry of Robinson Jeffers.* Copyright 1935 by Robinson Jeffers. Copyright © 1965 by Donnan Jeffers and Garth Jeffers. Reprinted by permission of Random House, Inc.

"Salvage," *The Beginning and the End and Other Poems.* Copyright © 1963 by Donnan Jeffers and Garth Jeffers. Reprinted by permission of Random House, Inc.

Letter from Robinson Jeffers published in the Carmel (California) *Pine Cone,* July 20, 1949. Reprinted by permission of *Pine Cone.*

Passage from letter to Melba Bennett from Mrs. Lee M. Jeffers, December 1956. Reprinted by permission of Mrs. Lee M. Jeffers.

Big Sur and the Oranges of Hieronymous Bosch by Henry Miller. Copyright © 1957 by New Directions Publishing Corporation. Reprinted by permission of New Directions Publishing Corporation.

"By Nigot," *American Indian Poetry,* edited by George Cronyn. Copyright renewed © 1962 by George Cronyn. Reprinted by permission of Liveright, New York.

A Coney Island of the Mind by Lawrence Ferlinghetti. Copyright © 1958 by New Directions Publishing Corporation. Reprinted by permission of New Directions Publishing Corporation.

"The Fragile Sea," words and music by Malvina Reynolds. Copyright © 1973 by Schroder Music Company (ASCAP). Reprinted by permission of Schroder Music Company (ASCAP).

I Cover the Waterfront by Max Miller. Copyright 1932 by E. P. Dutton & Co., Inc. Renewed © 1960 by Max Miller. Published by E. P. Dutton & Co., Inc., and used with their permission.

The Log from the Sea of Cortez by John Steinbeck. Copyright 1941 by John Steinbeck and Edward F. Ricketts. Copyright © renewed 1969 by John Steinbeck and Edward F. Ricketts, Jr. Copyright 1951 by John Steinbeck. Reprinted by permission of the Viking Press, Inc.

Published, 1974, in the United States by E. P. Dutton & Co., Inc., New York,
and simultaneously in Canada by Clarke, Irwin & Co., Ltd., Toronto and Vancouver

First Edition

All rights reserved under International and Pan-American Copyright Conventions

ISBN: 0-525-17438-9

Printed and bound in Japan by Dai Nippon Printing Co., Ltd.

Library of Congress Cataloging in Publication Data

Brokaw, Dennis.
  The Pacific shore.

  Bibliography: p.
  1. Nature conservation—Pacific coast (North America)
  2. Natural history—Pacific coast (North America)
  3. Pacific coast (North America)   I. Marx, Wesley,
  joint author. II. Title.
  QH77.P33B76   333.7′8′0979   74 10667

All photographs are by Dennis Brokaw except the following: pp. 11, 42, 86, Oregon Historical Society; pp. 33, 62, California State Library; p. 49, Title Insurance and Trust Company (Historical Collection), Los Angeles; p. 58, Free Lance Photographers Guild Inc.: Werner Stoy; p. 91, Henry E. Huntington Library and Art Gallery; p. 113, U.S. Geological Survey; p. 120, UPI; p. 124, U.S. Forest Service; and p. 125, Collections of Greenfield Village and the Henry Ford Museum, Dearborn, Michigan.

ACKNOWLEDGMENTS

I am grateful to Dr. John Mohr, of the University of Southern California, and to Dr. Joel Hedgpeth, director of the Marine Science Center, at Oregon State University, who read portions of the manuscript and made many helpful suggestions. They also brought helpful references to my attention.

Dr. Paul Rudy, director of the University of Oregon's Institute of Marine Biology, in arranging for a lecture assignment, provided me with the opportunity for an extended visit to the Oregon shore. Mr. John Marckx made available his summer residence near Willipa Bay, Washington, for an extended stay. Mr. William Press, executive director of the Planning and Conservation League, arranged for me to attend the 1973 California Ocean Pollution Conference at Lake Arrowhead, California. Members of the staff of the main library of the University of California at Irvine, an invaluable source of general reference material, were most cooperative. I am also indebted for support and encouragement to Richard Baisden, director of the University of California Extension at Irvine, and to Mrs. Ada Mae Hardeman and Mrs. Alice Anderson for developing courses on marine affairs. Mr. Gordon Enk, of the Institute of Man and Science at Rensselaerville, New York, arranged for me to attend the 1973 Invitational Symposium on Assessment of the Social Impacts of Oil Spills.

Mrs. Arlene Terris and my wife, Judy, typed the final manuscript, rescuing me in the process from my bent for phonetic spelling.

CONTENTS

THE PACIFIC SHORE

Chapter 1

The Nature of the Shore

God, Michelangelo, and the Scripps Institution of Oceanography have been suggested as likely designers of the Pacific shore. But I nominate Faust. For what is astounding about the region is its ability to bring out both the best and worst in human nature.

What goes into the design of a Faustian shore, one that intimidates seamen and inspires poets? Rolling combers and golden bluffs separated by thin strands of sand, massive headlands girt with mantling forests, a coast emerging in bright sun and receding in thick fog, sometimes set into vibration by earthquakes or awash in seismic sea waves. It is strewn with life that dazzles the already awestruck: teeming seal rookeries, seabird colonies, the world's tallest trees, the ocean's most prolific seaweeds, its largest and most delectable marine snail, and clams six inches across.

Salmon appear at the appointed moment and converge in river mouths in three feet of glass-clear water. On moonlit summer nights, glittering silvery sheets of grunion rise from the ocean, wriggle clear of the surf and cover the beaches, spawning. On tidal mudflats, a mere rake of the hand may uncover five or six juicy littleneck clams. I can send my six-year-old daughter to a nearby bay with a clam pail and she will return with supper. For this is a shore eager to take care of every want. Trees are grown as if to meet a lumberman's specifications. Tall. Straight. No untidy branches. Oil seeps

proclaim black treasure hidden thousands of feet underground. It is a shore that exudes strength, vitality, resources—challenging men with saws, nets, drills, and dredges.

Yet there is risk within this woven abundance. Each fiber and strand—coastal forest, sea forest, rock and sand—supports all the others. If the mesh is carelessly unraveled, salmon, beach and technological ingenuity vanish together. This exuberant environment is thus both life-sustaining and life-constraining.

Finally, to sharpen the human penchant for exploitation, most men are kept away until the time when ability to exploit has outraced their ability to control exploitation. You have then a Faustian shore, from Puget Sound to San Diego Bay. A shore ideally suited to encourage us to outsmart ourselves. Or improve on our planetary manners. For people more accustomed to changing the environment than their own perspectives, this can be a richly ironic experience. People in bathing suits and suntan lotion may compete zealously to exclude one another from walking a beach or watching an ocean sunset, some by using wire fences, others by using wire-cutters. Yet, given due respect, the Pacific shore reveals to us values more priceless and timeless than timber, oil, or exclusive views of the sunset. And it also reveals that we ourselves possess an extraordinary potential to restore as well as deplete, to admire as well as despoil.

In lowland estuaries and wetlands, sea and land blend imperceptibly. Such calm meeting places are rare along the Pacific shore. Here land and sea appear to be upstaging each other in a contest of grandeur. Rugged coastal ranges and the tallest of all forests are thrust seaward by the land. The sea responds with tumbling combers, submarine forests of giant kelp, and an occasional seismic wave. This contest reaches a climax when rolling blue combers smash into rocky headlands with a blinding, re-splendent explosion of white spray. In this grand collision, sea and land each seem determined to hurl back the other's intrusion.

As early explorers saw it, the Pacific shore seemed to defy man's intrusion as well. Juan Rodriguez Cabrillo wrote after passing by the Santa Lucia Mountains of central California in 1542, "These are mountains which reach the sky and the sea beats upon them. When sailing along near land, it seemed as if the mountains would fall upon the ships." For sailors exhausted by scurvy, diarrhea, and their own anxiety, the wall of mountains seemed unending. In fact, along its entire 1700-mile-length, the Pacific shore has only three natural harbors. A number of river mouths do cut through this intimidating coast, but these are just as in-timidating as coastal bluffs. In 1841, U. S. Com-mander Charles Wilkes wrote of the bar-trapped entrance to the Columbia River: "Mere descrip-tion can give little idea of the terrors of the bar. All who have seen it have spoken of the wildness of the sea and the incessant roar of the waters, representing it as one of the most fearful sights that can possibly meet the eye."

Travel on land was no less trying. In 1828, an explorer named Jedediah Strong Smith struggled among the coastal ranges of northern California.

> For a long time I had been traveling the country where our utmost exertions would not enable us to travel more than three miles per day at most, where my horses were mangled by the craggy rocks of the mountains over which they passed and suf-fered so much from hunger that I found myself under the necessity of stopping a while to rest them or run the risk of losing many of them if I should proceed.

Even today, in an age of jet lag and "sig" alerts, you can stand on a treeless bluff in southern Cali-fornia or on a forested cliff in Oregon, watch the silent parade of waves below, feel ocean breezes brighten your cheeks, and still share in Cabrillo's awe. If you can find your way down the bluff, you will hear the crack of the breaking waves and the slosh of surf against sand. A surfer may be riding a wave crest, as if delegated to escort the wave shoreward to its demise. You may plow through the churning surf yourself to the blue-green zone of wave swells, to swim towards the shore just as the right wave begins to steepen. Soon your own mo-tion is superseded by wave motion, leaving you suspended in the moving water, with surf sounds filling your ears as the shore rushes towards you. And then the sound and the motion cease, the wave is reduced to a swath of receding surf and you stand in the shadow of towering bluffs whose silent countenance glowers at the Pacific Ocean and at you.

Yet for all its massiveness, the coast range is no less awesome for its instability. You can't go to the bluff edge at your own leisure and discover this aspect of its character. But that character may reveal itself unannounced. One morning I awoke early when the bed beneath me began gently oscil-lating with the motion of a cresting wave. Opening my eyes I could see the walls sway silently, as if heeding a distant drumbeat. Moments later, I sat stunned with my wife and children before the tele-vision set, seeing hospitals split apart, freeway over-passes snapped like so many twigs, and concrete bridges shredded into ribbons. The scene, which seemed worlds away, was only sixty miles to the north. Closer to its epicenter in the northern Los Angeles area, the earthquake that had only rocked us gently had left people dead and buildings in ruins. The Pacific shore is part of a seismic belt that extends in a huge arc from New Zealand through the Philippines and Japan to the Aleutians and along the Pacific coast to Chile, and is so called because of the relative frequency of earthquakes, volcanic eruptions, and tsunamis—or seismic sea waves. About four-fifths of the world's earthquakes occur within this belt. According to the U. S. Geological Survey, in historical times earthquakes here have taken half a million lives. Such instability has been related to the theory of continental drift. According to this theory, the continents once formed one large land mass, which split apart into shifting geologic plates. Where these plates meet, one may drive over or under the other, and the result may be a deep marine trench, a mountain range, a volcano, or a geologic fault. The San Andreas Fault, which runs most of the length of California, appears to be the meeting place of two such plates. The part of California lying to the west of this fault line (including San Diego and Los Angeles) is slowly migrating northward. The San Francisco peninsula happens to be bisected by the fault and an abrupt movement along it was what triggered the 1906 earthquake. Seismic activity not only lifted the coastal mountains and the Cascade and Sierra Nevada ranges farther inland, but also played a part in trapping huge deposits of oil beneath the earth's surface.

And this geologic restlessness leaves scars—not only faults but also slide areas where the soils are loosely compacted. Such young and tortured landscapes can move abruptly, even without a seismic nudge. Some 3800 landslides over 100 feet in their largest dimension have been mapped in the Los Angeles-Orange County coastal basin area. In no more than a few seconds, the earthquake that woke me so gently triggered a thousand slides in the Los Angeles area and, by fracturing ridgetops, set the stage for as many more. Although California is more prone to seismic activity than Washington and Oregon, these coastal neighbors are by no means immune. Between 1840 and 1965, 850 earthquakes were recorded in Washington, the largest and most damaging in the Puget Sound region.

The coast ranges have been lifted into the path of rain clouds and fog drifting eastward from the Pacific Ocean. Anywhere from sixty to ninety inches of rain drench the Oregon coast each year. Such downpours could dissolve young and unstable mountain ranges. However, the roots of the world's tallest trees help bind together the ranges along the Pacific shore. Redwoods, Douglas firs, and cedars rise straight and true as a million ship masts. Spruces tower bristling like sentries next to the drooping, shawllike limbs of the more sinuous hemlock. Southward, where rainfall tapers off, Robinson Jeffers' elfin forests of chaparral are dominant. Though stunted in appearance, the evergreen chaparral is just as effective as the tall redwoods and cedars in anchoring the mountain slopes against massive erosion.

Fire is integral to these coastal forests, clearing off collected underbrush and permitting new growth. Even amid the damp forests of the north, lightning or sparks caused by friction with a falling tree can ignite such a growth-renewing blaze. "The country around us is all on fire. The weather is gloomy from the smoke around us," wrote one British explorer from the Pacific Northwest.

Much of the moisture carried by the Pacific to the coastal ranges flows back to the ocean over numerous coastal watersheds. The majestic, long-flowing rivers of the Gulf coast and the Atlantic seaboard are rare along the Pacific slope. The Sacramento and American river system and the Columbia, which stretches for 1400 miles and rises in the Canadian icefields, are the principal exceptions. Most watersheds begin at the crest of the coastal ranges, weaving, bobbing, jumping, and darting downward through the steep landscape to merge rather abruptly with the Pacific Ocean. Some of these coastal rivers begin and end within the eyesight of an observer. The flow from such steeply tilted watersheds can be highly variable—swollen by winter rains or starved under clear summer skies. Many southern California rivers appear to be nothing but a prank, weaving linear deserts most of the year. Yet the runoff from rain percolates through these riverbeds to form extensive groundwater reservoirs in the semiarid coastal plains.

The watersheds of the Pacific slope are integral to marine processes, as are the tides. Salmon rise from mid-Pacific depths to converge on river mouths and return to ancestral spawning places. Besides returning young salmon to the Pacific, the coastal rivers deliver another essential cargo: grains of feldspar and quartz. These grains serve as replenishment for beaches five miles long and dunes two stories high. A slurry of sand extends from mountain crests down creekbeds and along the littoral, continually renewing wave-pounded beaches. Waves that batter sandstone bluffs into sandy tailings augment the riverine transport of sand. Eroding sandstone bluffs can become the material of wind-blown sand dunes farther down the coast. Such geological subversion produces massive silicon streams. Every year an estimated one million cubic yards of sand moves off Port Hueneme in southern California. Along the Oregon coast, wind-blown sand nourishes dune fields that constitute a minor coastal range. The dunes become a moving landscape, edging inland, overwhelming coastal forests and here and there blocking the course of a stream to form a lake.

The close interplay between sea and land is probably best seen in the California Current. Partly as a result of the earth's rotation, the vanguard of the Pacific Ocean piles up against the Asian coast, generating a current that moves northward along the coast of Japan, eastward below the Aleutians, and then southeast along the American continent, where it becomes the California Current. As winds move warm air over it, moist clouds form and move inland. Cooler temperatures condense the vapor and drench the coastal forests. In summer the clouds diminish. As temperatures rise, however, the warmer air becomes charged with water vapor, which condenses into summer fog. The fog permits coastal forests to survive in the summer heat. Point Reyes in California is mantled by dense fogs 148 days of a year. Combined with the rugged coast, the fogs make the Pacific shore a navigator's nightmare. Chaplin Francis Fletcher complained to Sir Francis Drake on his 1579 stopover on the California coast of "those thick mists and most striking fogges . . . where a blind pilot is as good as the best director of a course." Navigators are continually torn between their eagerness to see landmarks on the rocky, fog-obscured headlands, and their wariness of colliding with other ships or foundering on rocky shoals.

The California Current helps explain why summer swimmers upcoast of southern California find the ocean waters so cold that they turn away from the shore in favor of rafting down the warm coastal rivers. The coolness of the current is not solely the result of having passed through the Gulf of Alaska. Another cause can be traced to the prevailing northwest winds which tend to push surface water away from the coast so that cold bottom water rises to replace the surface water. This vertical displacement is known as upwelling, and the eastern Pacific coast is one of the most notable regions where it occurs. Upwelling is primarily a phenomenon of the early spring and summer, when the chilling of the water produces the summer fogs that mask the coastal forests.

Upwelling is vital to the productivity of both sea and land. The mountainous Pacific shore is not as rich in fertile estuarine areas as the Gulf or the Atlantic. Much of the productivity of the Pacific shore depends on the plankton, tiny plants and animals that are the "pastures of the sea." The growth of plankton can deplete the surface water of nutrients—and without a continuing supply of these, the water becomes relatively infertile. But the cold bottom waters brought to the surface by upwelling help to renew the supply. In coastal regions where upwelling occurs, there can be rich marine crops. At times, indeed, their planktonic richness can appear suicidal—as when deadly "blooms" of certain planktonic species become so dense that the body pigments of these microscopic creatures literally dye the ocean brick red, in what is known as the "red tide."

To one familiar only with the clumps of seaweed swarming with beach fleas that have washed ashore on the beach, the idea of seaweed growing in dense forests on the ocean floor may seem unlikely. Nevertheless, this is literally true. Along the rim of the Pacific shore brown kelp rises from bottom anchorages or holdfasts in vinelike fronds that form a thick brown canopy at the surface of the waters. Fronds of the giant brown kelp are known to cover an area of eight square miles. These forests are generally within reach of anyone who swims past the surf zone, since they generally grow at depths of one hundred feet or less.

In a sea forest, the struggle for existence is waged at every level. Seabirds dive-bomb for smelt through canopy openings, and sea otters fatten on spiny sea urchins that graze among the kelp holdfasts on the ocean floor.

Descending for the first time into a sea forest can be a disconcerting experience. The silent, swaying fronds of kelp appear ready to reach out and snare an intruder. Then you see fish of every size and color gliding nonchalantly through openings in the foliage, and soon you are doing the same. Whereas the wild life of a land forest are sent scampering at the first crack of a twig, the dwellers of a sea forest seem undismayed by your presence. You look an ocean perch in the eye only to be outstared in turn. Schools of smelt pass in total unconcern like a shower of rain. What appears to be a flame in search of its source is a garibaldi, the goldfish of the ocean.

When the thick surface canopy cuts off sunlight from the young bottom fronds, the mature fronds at the surface pass down their energy to them in a process called translocation. With its young fronds adding as much as two feet a day, kelp is one of the fastest-growing plants on the planet. The life of a single frond is short; after about seven months it weakens, breaks off, and is eventually washed onto a beach—where, despised by bathers, it becomes a haven for beach fleas.

The plankton pastures of the California Current, the kelp forests near the shore, and the intertidal shellfish beds are traversed by salmon, seals, seabirds, and other migratory species. The seemingly abrupt line between land and sea that dismayed Cabrillo and that continues to awe us is in fact crisscrossed by life-giving processes that link redwood forests and ocean currents in a close comradeship. Yet this interplay is so subdued, so unobtrusive that one can remain quite oblivious to it. My parents brought me to the Pacific shore as a child with sandpail in hand. I learned to build sand castles, to fish, and to body surf, and collected driftwood for countless sunset cookouts. But I learned little about the Pacific shore itself. I saw it as glamorous yet static, a natural backdrop that was simply to be taken for granted. I began to learn how mistaken this notion was only by accident, when my wife and I were living in a base-ment apartment along the Malibu shore. We were planning to have a beach party, and awoke on the appointed day to find the beach gone, leaving only exposed rocks: the shore had let us down. My wife, undaunted, put me to shoveling sand over the protruding rocks. A high tide proceeded to remove the results of my labor, and our beach party became an outing on a rocky shore. But within a week the beach returned . . . without my assistance. After that, I no longer took the Pacific shore for granted. I began to read about, and to observe for myself, the interplay between erosive storm waves and the beach-building waves of summer. I discovered that the main source of beaches was not the ocean but the mountain watersheds a hundred miles inland. The shore that had once seemed so neatly compartmentalized into land and water was now a place throbbing with huge cross-currents of energy, with tides moving in and out, with beaches that periodically contracted and expanded, with rivers that shrank and then swelled again, with coastal fogs and redwood forests as closely intermeshed as the mechanism of a watch. Instead of regarding the shore as a backdrop, I began to have a sense that I was living inside some immense natural engine that was made up not only of the beach outside our apartment but also of the sky above and the mountains beyond. The sheer magnitude of this engine conjured up images of gears meshing, of steel moving against steel, of towering smokestacks, revolving turbines, and the shriek of steam whistles. The effects it produced seemed to call for the presence of engineers, the attention of mechanics, and the infusion of vast quantities of lubricating oil to keep the whole thing in operation. And yet it involves none of these things—not even noise.

The shore I once took for granted is now a source of continual wonder and fascination. One can never learn enough about it—about the waves, the beaches, the offshore forests of kelp, or about such details as the ability of the sun-drenched chaparral to hoard sparse moisture in its leatherlike leaves or the seastar to extrude its stomach into a mussel's shell and digest the creamy flesh inside. If you seek an answer to a question—about the color of a sand beach, for example—you may wind up on a pine-shaded mountain slope where gravel crunches underfoot.

Yet this deep-running and extensive interplay of natural forces is obscured by the clear-cut divisions of sea and land, beach and bluff, city limits and state borders, by signs that say No Trespassing and Beware the Dog.

Early white explorers were dazzled by the sheer exuberance of life along the Pacific coast. John Rickman, sailing with Captain James Cook in 1778, told how one day "we were alarmed by the clashing of the waves, as if some great building was tumbling in, and, looking round the ship, we saw ourselves involved among shoals of seals and sea lions, who presently set up the most frightful howlings that possibly can be conceived. . . ." A few days later he wrote, "The men were employed in fishing, and in less than four hours caught more than three ten weight of cod and halibut, some of the latter more than a 100 pounds weight." Only a month before, with food stores depleted by their long voyage, these men had dined on a "fricassee of rats . . . whenever they could be lucky enough to catch a number sufficient to make a meal." Nor were one-hundred-pound halibut the only prizes the North Pacific coast yielded up to starved mariners. "The men had then leave to go ashore, by turns, to gather berries, which they now found ripe and in great abundance, such as raspberries, blue-

berries, black and red currants, huckleberries, with various other sorts, all in full perfection. A party was likewise sent out to cut spruce to brew into beer." A slight dissent was registered here: "Of this liquor, however, the men were not very fond in this cold climate. . . . This occasioned great murmuring, and it was found necessary to give it alternately, spruce one day and grog another."

Unhappily, natural abundance can be seen as a license for exploitation. Having feasted on halibut and blueberries, Cook's men came across more seal herds along the icy Alaskan coast. Almost by instinct they grabbed for their muskets.

This by the sailors was accounted sport; and they went to the attack with as much alacrity as if to a match at football. Orders were given, as soon as the great guns were discharged, to quicken the attack with the musketry as fast as possible. In a few minutes not a creature was to be seen upon the ice but such as were killed or so severely wounded as not to be able to crawl to the open sea. Some lay growling on the ice not quite dead, with two or three balls through their heads, and others tumbling about with horrible vindictive looks, threatening destruction to whoever should approach them.

Subjected to this compulsion, the natural productivity of the Pacific shore would become both a blessing and a curse. Indeed for a full comprehension of this abundance, one must go back to the dim records of another culture.

THE MEETING

A wave bursts in anger on a rock, broken up in a wild white sibilant spray and falls back, drawing in its breath with rage, with frustration . . .
—D. H. Lawrence

Broad, unobstructed expanses of ocean create a type of "Pacific" wave action far more powerful than that experienced along the Atlantic coast. This "wave shock"—the strongest in the Northern Hemisphere—batters exposed beaches from Cape Flattery, northwest of Seattle, Washington, south to Pt. Conception, near Santa Barbara, California.

(right) Sea Lion Rocks, Pt. Lobos, California. "Smoking mountains," Robinson Jeffers called the great waves of winter. "Often I first hear them at night, in the upstairs room of our house at Carmel. Heavy as thunder, but more powerful, somehow seeming to shake the ground as they pound on the sand beach of Carmel Bay."

Crescent City, California. It was here that the tidal wave struck.

(right) Rocky Creek, Big Sur, California. The wind does its share of beach construction, blasting away at hills and bluffs; the swirling, eddying surf distributes the sand.

Sea Lion Cove, Pt. Lobos.

(right) Near Ecola State Park, Oregon. The last keeper of the offshore light (now automated) reported seas rolling over the light 139 feet above mean sea level during a winter storm. On Columbus Day, 1965, the winds here blew steadily at 170 mph.

Low tide, Torrey Pines Park, north of La Jolla, California.

(left) Boardman State Park, Oregon. The Oregon coast is almost entirely of volcanic origin. Jagged basaltic rocks, remnants of ancient volcanic flows and cones, dot the shore. To see it at its best, without heavy fog, go inland—just before sunset—to a high point of land.

Anacapa Island, Santa Barbara Channel Islands, California. Anacapa is out of character with either the larger Channel Islands or the sedimentary terraces of the mainland coast. Beds of giant kelp surround the volcanic island, sheltering great schools of anchovies and other forage fish, which in turn support countless marine organisms. Mammals, sea birds, and migrating silver şalmon from the Pacific Northwest are common.

(right) There is a time of seasonal change along the central California coast when the persistent fogs of summer have abated and the storm fronts of winter have not yet begun. During the fall at Carmel and along the Big Sur coast, spectacular sunsets are commonplace events. The degree of sky brilliance is unpredictable until a moment or two before the sun seems to drop.

Monterey cypress with lichen above Pinnacle Cove.

(left) Cypress and granite, Pt. Lobos. The Monterey cypress seems to edge inexorably westward into the sea, to its own extinction. These gnarled, convoluted trees are made by the "sailor wind" that Jeffers spoke of, with its knottying propensities.

(overleaf) Olympic National Park, Washington. The cold ocean wind keeps beaches on the west side of the Olympic Peninsula cool and foggy.

Crescent City, California.

(right) Near Samuel Boardman Memorial, Boardman State Park. The ferocious sea wind's "shrubbery," mostly Sitka spruce trees, are raked flat by winter storms. The same spruce, sheltered in the rain forests of the Olympic Peninsula, grow almost as large as the giant redwoods.

Bluefish Cove, Pt. Lobos. Like Monterey cypress, Monterey pine vary in appearance, depending on where they grow. Here they grow tall, but spare and angular in sea fogs and northwest winds; succulents, called stonecrop or bluff lettuce, sprout among fallen needles or from crevices between granite rocks.

Chapter 2

Natives of the Pacific Shore

Though most of the coastal Indians are gone from California you may still happen upon their traces. Here and there along the pale bluffs overlooking Upper Newport Bay in southern California are patches of green foliage, where the pitch-dark soil is still flecked with shells left behind by the Indians centuries ago. On lonely San Miguel Island in the Santa Barbara Channel, quantities of abalone shells and stone pestles, scoured by sandstorms, are proof that Indians once lived there. At the Los Angeles Museum of Natural History is a miniature killer whale carved out of soapstone, its mouth curled in an enigmatic smile.

We know—or think we know—much about the Aztec, the Maya, and the Plains Indians—about their dress and their myths, about such heroes as Sitting Bull, Crazy Horse, Geronimo, and Montezuma. But the California coastal Indians have made little impression on the popular imagination. They didn't ride horses, put up wigwams or go on scalping expeditions.

California contains 5 percent of the land area in the entire United States. Large parts of it, such as Death Valley, are barely habitable. Yet the densest Indian settlements in the United States—some 130,000 people, or an estimated 16 percent of the total Indian population—flourished in California, mainly along the coast. (Recent findings have caused some anthropologists to project a population twice as large.) These people were dis-

tinctive in that they lived by hunting and still had plenty of leisure.

The land, the coastal rivers, and the sea were all so rich in food that these Indians had little reason to farm, go to war, or pray for rain. Unlike the plains Indians, who lived primarily by hunting buffalo, the California Indians had a choice of salmon, oysters, clams, sardines, acorns, bulbs, roots, berries, seeds, grasshoppers and seal meat. They were unimpressed by the jerked beef that gave subsistence to early white visitors. "They do not enjoy our food and drink so much. Although they took it out of politeness, they threw it away when we were not looking," noted one eighteenth-century Spanish visitor, Don Juan Francisco Bodega y Quadra.

With the interface between land and sea offering such variety, these native Californians could harvest whatever food was most readily available. They became students of natural history, experts on biological rhythms: they knew when oaks were bearing acorns, when the salmon were running, when the seals were in their rookeries, when to look for shellfish exposed by low tides in the estuaries, and for abalone, the largest of marine snails, on the rocky shore. A California Indian had no need for complicated mechanisms of harvest or extraction, he didn't have to plant or cultivate. He went about among the forests and valleys with a digging stick and an incredible store of information about what plants and tubers were edible. His diet included anywhere from fifty to a hundred different plants, from sage to agave bulbs. He used cactus to "chum" (attract) fish, and dip nets to bring in congregating sardines or smelts. He used the bone of a whale to pry away the abalone that had clamped its foot onto the rocks, and tenderized the cream-colored meat he found inside its iridescent shell with a cobblestone from the beach. To make fishing easier, he concocted a mash of buckeye nuts and the root of the soap plant and threw it into the creek whose waters had been dammed up temporarily. Stupefied by the mash, the fish could be scooped up by the hundreds.

When it came to boats, the same ingenuity prevailed. Birch bark canoes or balsa rafts would have been too flimsy for plowing through the surf. But more rugged materials were at hand—logs and other heavy driftwood, split into planks with wedges of rock and whalebone, were sewn together with deer sinew or leather cut into strips by clam shells, and made waterproof by caulking with tar from the asphalt seeps that are so abundant in California, particularly in the area of the Santa Barbara Channel. (The caulking compound was also used as chewing gum.) Paddles were fashioned with a blade at each end to conserve motion in switching from one side of the craft to the other. These canoes, light yet sturdy, made it possible for the Chumash tribe to colonize the Channel Islands one hundred miles offshore. As many as two thousand Indians lived on the small islands of San Miguel and San Nicolas, which were among the densest of all Indian settlements in North America. Spanish explorers who came ashore soaking wet from landing in the surf were impressed by the Indians' plank canoes. An entry in the ship diary of Sebastián Vizcaíno reads, "Five Indians came in another canoe so well constructed and built that since Noah's Ark a finer and lighter vessel with timbers better made has not been seen."

The plank canoes enabled the Chumash Indians to harvest the rich populations of fish in the submarine kelp forests that fringed the coast. Hooks carved out of abalone shell were attached to a kelp stem, with a notched stone as a sinker. Strands of kelp wound around the paddle functioned as a handhold. The canoe would often be moored to a kelp plant. An understanding of the coastal environment thus brought rewards. Father Crespi reported of a visit to one California coastal village:

As soon as we arrived all the people came to visit us and brought us a great supply of roasted fish to eat until the canoes should arrive with fresh ones. They soon landed on the beach, and in a little while afterwards they brought us an abundance of bonitas and perch, which they gave us in such quantities that we could have loaded the entire pack train if we had any means of preparing and salting them. They gave us also fish dried without salt, which they do not use in their food.

In their own way, these Indians were no less adept than the Polynesians at living from the sea. They were good swimmers, using a sidearm stroke. Provided with a tide pool, driftwood, and an asphalt seep, they flourished with far greater ease than inland tribes. Rather than horses they rode the Pacific itself.

The bounty of the Pacific coast, and the cleverness of the Indians in exploiting this bounty removed one principal cause of strife: scarcity of food resources. When there was such abundance, highly organized tribal systems prepared to retaliate against the slightest infringment of their territory made little sense. In fact, California Indians often identified themselves with the place they inhabited rather than with the tribe they belonged to. This insularity generated a babel of dialects—an estimated total of 135 were spoken by various groups of California Indians. Spanish translators found this fragmentation exhausting; one declared the Indian groups along the coast to be "mutually unintelligible."

Such wars as did break out were often no more than quarrels among kinsmen—often the only level at which people could even understand each other.

Although bows and spears were used, the nearest available stone was just as likely to be the major weapon. The practice of scalping was unheard of until it was brought in by another culture.

The mild California climate made an extensive wardrobe unnecessary, and in this the Indians of the region did not go out of their way to improve on nature. The men often went entirely naked, donning sealskin capes only in colder weather. Exposing the body to sun and wind was thought to discourage lice, as well as to toughen the skin until the bite of a flea was a mere prick. Deer fat was used to ward off sunburn. Women wore a two-piece skirt of skin or fiber with tiny balls of asphalt tied to the ends to keep them from blowing up in the sea breeze. Surf grass was twisted into mats that served as bedding. Shredded sage bark, crisp and pungent, was used to make baby diapers. The mild climate also made shelter a simple matter—a small hut of matted tule reeds, perhaps with whale ribs arched to form a door, and with clean beach sand as a carpet.

By taking such resourceful advantage of their coastal environment, the California coastal Indians avoided any unnecessary expenditure of energy on the traditional pursuits of food gathering and war. They approached the leisure that was made possible with gusto. They loved decoration in all forms. Out of shells they made jewelry; out of minerals they manufactured paint; out of asphalt they made glue. The iridescent abalone shell went into earrings. To carry the clanking cargo of abalone shell, seal teeth, and stone pendants, the ear itself might be pierced six times. The only plant these Indians cultivated—tobacco—was for pleasure rather than sustenance. They grew it in village refuse heaps. Canoes plying to and from Catalina Island brought soapstone from its three hundred quarries—raw material for tobacco pipes and for carving miniature smiling killer whales. Deposits of hematite and cinnabar yielded red pigment for painting faces and canoes; black paint was made of charcoal.

The urge to decorate was not restricted to *objets d'art*, but was part of living. The Pomo Indians excelled in basketry. They used fibers from sedge, willows, and spruce and rosebud shoots, to weave spherical containers tight enough to hold water, decorating them with dazzling geometric designs in red and black. Feather mosaics were sometimes added: the red scalps of woodpeckers from the redwood forests, the yellow breasts of orioles and green from the heads of mallard ducks. Today these baskets, some no larger than your thumb, are cherished in museums throughout the world.

The body itself was prominently decorated. At a distance, noted a Spanish missionary, the Indians of the San Francisco Bay area "appeared to be dressed in striped cloth." In fact the stripes consisted of body paint in bold patterns of black, red, and white. The face would be tattooed in concentric lines that converged at mid-chin.

The esthetic impulse that adorned their daily life spilled over into music. The Viscaíno ship diary describes how in one Chumash canoe, "four men rowed, with an old man at the center, singing as in a 'nitote' of the Indians of New Spain, and the others responding to him." After nightfall the singers might become dancers, since their folklore warned of a day when the earth might tip into the ocean and whales ascend the river as easily as salmon. To ward off this catastrophe, there were marathons of dancing and foot-stomping. In another dance, the Chumash donned swordfish masks in the hope of bringing in a supply of blubber, since whales stranded on the beach were thought to have been chased ashore by swordfish.

Sometimes the men would retire to a sweathouse, the *temescal,* where they would lather their bodies with the crushed blossoms of the wild lilac and scrape off the perspiration with the jawbone of a porpoise. Then, after trading gossip for a while they would dash out to cool themselves in a stream or the Pacific surf and take a sunbath. The missionary Pedro Font observed, "These Indians are well-formed and of good body, although not very corpulent on account of their sweating, I judge." With their natural affluence, these Indians were more apt to work up a sweat in this sociable way than in pursuit of a livelihood.

Other Indians flourished along the North Pacific coast, from near Cape Mendocino in California northward into south Alaska. Like the California Indians, they were hunters with leisure to develop arts and entertainment. Responding to a coastal environment that saw less of the sun, they evolved their own distinctive cultures.

Like the California Indians, those of the North Pacific closely studied the behavior of their quarry, chief of which was the salmon. When they migrated from the ocean depths to the river mouths along the coast, the salmon were met by an array of lethal devices, among which the baited hook was not very prominent. Entering a bay or river mouth on an ebbing tide, they might encounter shallow bars or tidal flats. To avoid becoming stranded, they would move to deeper channels, only to be blocked once again—this time by stone fences which the low tide had exposed. The waiting Indians would then use dip nets to bring in the trapped fish. Salmon that avoided this tidal trap might encounter a long series of river barriers that funneled them at last into bags of webbing. Along the Klamath River, where the Yurok Indians lived, still other salmon would catch their heads in a submerged net that snagged them by the gills as they tried frantically to back away.

Salmon are agile enough to clear small waterfalls. Some may lengthen their jump sufficiently to hurdle a barrier at the base of the falls. Such a barrier may make the jump too long, however, and when the fish falls back, it is only to be caught in a trap set by the same Indian who installed the barrier. There are still other Indians who may net a salmon in the midst of a jump. The Dalles region on the Columbia River remains notable to this day as a place for waterfall ambushes. Salmon that have evaded gill nets, tidal corrals, and waterfall traps may rest in an eddy or a quiet pool before advancing upriver to spawn in the streams of their birth. Here, in the quiet, clear water, harpooners would be waiting.

A few days spent at the nearest waterfall or river mouth could free an Indian from the demands of food gathering over the next four or five months. Once the fishing was done, his womenfolk would cut the salmon into strips, dry it in the sun, and then smoke it. At the Dalles, fishing was so good

that Indian groups from as far away as the Great Plains would come to trade pelts for a part of the catch. Thanks to the abundance of salmon, the Chinook Indians at the Dalles were the biggest traders in the far west.

The Indians did not take the salmon for granted. The first one caught was sprinkled with eagle down and displayed at an altar. It was believed that a menstruating girl would offend or discourage the salmon from coming and she would be sequestered. (According to one folk tale, once a girl was so bored with being confined that she looked out and taunted a nearby glacier by waving a piece of salmon at it. In response the glacier then moved, sweeping away the girl along with her entire village.)

Each year, a whole chain of First Salmon ceremonies progressed upriver along with the salmon run. Salmon eaters returned fishbones to the river so that the fish could renew themselves and return the next year.

A chief impatient over the arrival of the salmon might string together some skulls, jump into a river, and tow the skulls upstream. This was to entice the spirits of the dead to tow in the salmon from their home underneath the sea.

Bears were also enthusiastic followers of the salmon run and the North Pacific Indians had discovered ways to take advantage of this. Sometimes a bear would snatch at a salmon, only to be felled by a huge log, set at an angle, with the fish used as bait to trigger it for someone who wanted a bear-skin robe or cape.

When the salmon supply was low or had become rancid, the Indians would comb the shore at low tide, carrying baskets and hardwood sticks, which they used to pry up mussels and other shellfish. Herring and smelt that had come to spawn in the waters just offshore could sometimes be impaled by an Indian in a canoe, using an oar edged with spikes made of bone. Each time he made a catch, the Indian would pull in the oar, shake the fish onto the canoe bottom, and begin another impaling stroke, all in one continuous motion. Eggs spawned by the herring, adhering in sticky masses to seaweed, would also be harvested, and often fir branches would be strung in customary spawning places to make collection easier.

The agile feet of the Quinault Indians along the Washington coast often sufficed to ensnare flatfish in shallow bays, according to one nineteenth-century observer, James Swan:

> The Indian wades along slowly, and, as soon as he feels the fish with his feet, he steps quickly on it and holds it firmly until he can reach hold of it with his hand, when he gives it a jerk, and away it flies far into the flats. This process is repeated until enough fish are caught, when they are picked up, put in a basket, and carried to the canoe. They are easily taken by this method of the Indians, as their rough backs prevent them from slipping under the feet. The catching affords a deal of fun, as usually quite a number are engaged in the sport, and their splashing, slipping, screaming, and laughing make a lively time. These fish, like all the fish in the bay, are very fine and well flavored.

Occasionally a mother sea otter, having left her cub while she foraged for sea urchins or abalone below the surface, would return to find her cub gone. Hearing it squeal, she would swim towards it, only to be clubbed by an Indian, hidden in a canoe bottom or behind a rock on shore, who had taken the cub as a lure. The hunter would now be able to dress in an elegant cape of otterskin.

When otter and seals hauled up on their island rookeries at calving time, and gulls gathered in flocks to feed on the afterbirth, Indians would also gather to club the marine mammals. Trying to escape, a seal might slide down a rock ramp towards the surf, only to be impaled on sharp spruce points set by the Indians. These would contain detachable spearheads, which kept the squealing victim tethered until it could be clubbed.

On Cape Flattery, an Indian would sometimes swim into dark sea caverns that echoed with the bellowing seals. His hair would be wound and knotted atop his head to hold a flaming splint of pitchwood. Blinded by the light, the seals could be easily clubbed. The hunter would swim out of the cavern towing a string of five or six stunned seals attached to a thong held between his teeth.

Hook fishing expanded the horizons of food gathering. Bone hooks baited with octopus, dangled from a kelp stem with a wood block or an inflated seal bladder as a buoy, could snare a 200-pound halibut.

Waterfowl on the move along the Pacific flyway would be ensnared in the semidarkness by nets of willow bark as they swooped low over inland bays. Other ducks would be attracted to herring spawn, spread over seaweed that concealed a strategically placed net which snared the ducks as they dived below the surface. At night, the glow from a pitchwood flare in a canoe would lure the birds close enough to be captured with a net.

Although acorn-bearing oaks were not plentiful along the North Pacific coast, a woman might slip into the forest and return with berries of all sorts: salmon berries, salal berries, huckleberries, and blackberries. Clover, fern roots, and sea grass could be made into cakes, and crabapples could be boiled. However, because plant life was seasonal and couldn't be preserved easily, the Indians did not depend on plant food sources. To obtain oil, the Indians again relied on the sea, particularly clubbed seals, stranded whales, and on the eulachon, or candlefish. During its upstream migrations, tribes would converge on eulachon runs along what were called "grease trails," and women would press the fish to their breasts to squeeze out the oil. It was the Indians' equivalent of butter, in which they dipped dried salmon, halibut, herring eggs, berries, and fern roots.

As cooking pots, the Indians used baskets filled with water and red-hot stones. To steam clams open, fir boughs would sometimes be spread over red-hot stones, and water poured over the boughs. "This is much the best mode of cooking and clams and muscles [sic] done in this way are really excellent," wrote John Jewitt, a shipwreck survivor who was held captive by the Nootka Sound Indians during the 1820s. The saying that "When the tide is out, the table is set," is one these Indians understood very well.

The abundance of food helped counter boredom as well as hunger. When winter rains kept them from any other activity, there might be as many as eight meals a day to help pass the time.

Unlike the Mediterranean climate further south, that of the North Pacific coast brought cool temperatures plus rain, rain and still more rain. In such wetness, it was not possible to go without clothes. Leather breeches and breastplates would have been soggy most of the time. But in loose-fitting capes of seal and bearskin the Indians stayed dry and warm. The men wore very little underneath. Bare feet were favored over moccasins, since they withstood rain better. Conical basket hats helped keep off the rain, and to protect the skin from sunburn, ocean glare, frostbite, insects, and the blazing heat of lodge fires, body grease and decorative paint were used.

The Indians of the North Pacific coast built much roomier quarters than the California coastal Indians. In a rainy climate, mud huts roofed with reeds would not have lasted long. The soft, easily handled and even-grained nature of maritime redwood and cedar enabled the Indians to transform these giant trees into spacious lodges without the aid of tri-squares, levels and chain saws. For this purpose trees along the shore were generally shunned, since exposure to sunlight caused them to sprout more limbs and knots than the larger and "cleaner" trees that grew farther inland. The wind became their ally as the Indians went about the seemingly gigantic task of felling these trees. Stone wedges were driven into the tree above the butt swell, and another cut was made farther up the tree trunk. Then the Indians would wait patiently as the wind gradually broadened the cuts, eventually felling the tree. Then they used stone malls to split the wind-severed logs into planks, rafters, and corner poles. The planks overlapped to keep rain and wind out, and stones were placed on the roof to keep gusty southeast winds from blowing the lodge away. The Yurok lodges, as a special touch, had sliding plank doors, but were without either chimney or window. Roof planks were shifted about to admit light and let smoke out. Since the Indians burned green wood, there was a good deal of smoke—particularly in seasons when eight meals a day were being prepared. Fortunately cedar was also relatively fire-resistant.

Since they moved about with the seasons—from fishing and sealing grounds in the summer to salmon streams in the fall—the North Pacific Indians required two or three different dwellings—which in turn required a lot of cedar wood. Restoring to a kind of prefabrication, the Indians moved the sliding wall planks from one seasonal home to another, but left the corner poles and rafters standing.

As a nineteenth-century fur trapper, Peter Corney, debarked on the northern California coast, he heard voices coming from beneath his feet. "We found ourselves above an Indian Village," he reported, "for here they live underground and we could hear their voices beneath us." In these subterranean villages, wood was required only for the roofs.

The coast ranges discouraged overland movement. To carry a message up or down a three-thousand-foot slope and through the rain-soaked darkness of the forest was difficult enough; to transport salmon over the same route was a superhuman feat. The Indians relied on the water for transportation as well as for food. Instead of plank canoes, the North Pacific Indians built dugouts, using fire and stone adzes to begin hollowing out the logs. Next, the charred and chipped hollow was filled with water and steamed with hot rocks to soften up the wood. Thwarts could then be installed; these served to widen the beam by as much as a foot, and planks fitted along the edge of the dugout raised the waterboard. Finally, the dugout was singed and smoothed with dogfish skin. Avoiding the steep terrain, the Indians could cover forty miles a day in these dugouts. The exercise of paddling made their stocky bodies especially powerful in the upper torso and in the arms and shoulders.

In Oregon in 1856 Phil Sheridan, then a lieutenant looking for a site for a military post, found a bayfront covered with Indian burial canoes. Having persuaded the Indians of the area to agree to their removal, Sheridan's soldiers dispatched the ghostly fleet on a convenient ebb tide.

To obtain whale oil, the Indians most often waited until a whale conveniently stranded itself. But even though stalking thirty-ton whale offshore was not particularly inviting, the Nootka and Makah Indians did pursue whales that dwarfed their canoes. First they would emulate their huge prey, diving into freshwater ponds and emerging to blow out mouthfuls of water. The anthropologist Edward Curtis recorded one prayer before a whale hunt:

Whale, I want you to come near me, so that I will get hold of your heart and deceive it, so that I will have strong legs and not be trembling and excited when the whale comes and I spear him. Whale, you must not run out to sea when I spear you. Whale, if I spear you, I want my spear to strike your heart. Harpoon, when I use you, I want you to go to the heart of the whale. Whale, when I spear at you and miss you, I want you to take hold of my spear with your hands. Whale, do not break my canoe, for I am going to do good to you. I am going to put eagle-down and cedar bark in your back.

For stalking whales, the Nootka canoe was propelled by six oarsmen, with a harpooner in the bow. The harpoon itself was about twenty feet long and so heavy that the harpooner had to be maneuvered almost on top of the whale. The oarsman at the rudder seat was ready to back water to escape thrashing flukes. The blade, a mussel shell or a hemlock knot held in place by cedar fibers and spruce gum (there weren't many asphalt seeps in the north), might shatter on impact, but barbs of elk bone helped to secure the shaft. The whale began dragging at the harpoon line, made of cedar withes with a sealskin float to show its location. More harpoons would rain down on the wounded mammal, until it might be dragging forty or more sealskin floats. The accumulating floats chained it to the surface. As the whale neared exhaustion, canoers would maneuver in close. The tendons in the whale's flukes would be severed, thus destroying its ability to maneuver. The limp giant would then be towed ashore and covered with eagle down and cedar bark. Gray whales, with their affinity for nearshore water, were the prime target of these forays.

The North Pacific coast Indians were more war-like than their southern brethren. Apparently population pressures and the capricious movements of glaciers triggered group migrations which in turn led to territorial battles over salmon streams and seal rookeries. The canoe paddles wielded by their braves ended in a point—the better to put out the eye of an enemy at sea. The disfigured faces observed by early explorers testified to this fierce dual function. Slavery was not uncommon; raiding war parties from northern groups occasionally took captives from southern tribes. As a form of torture, a prisoner might be stretched out and staked to a mudflat at low tide, with the prospect of drowning when the tide came in again.

Like the California Indians, the North Pacific Indians enjoyed such natural abundance that they had ample leisure. Socially they were centered around kin groups; the tribes themselves were rather loosely organized. An entire kin group of up to a hundred might live together in one lodge, the babies playing, the women cooking salmon, the whale blubber dripping oil from the ceiling. Rank was based on wealth, heredity, or a combination of the two. Each person's particular rank, even within the family group, was carefully worked out and had to be scrupulously observed. To ignore anyone's particular rank was to risk igniting tempers. Publicizing one's rank could forestall such a clash.

For the Indians to the south, beauty and prestige were woven out of willow and sea grass fibers; for the North Pacific coast Indians, it was chipped and carved out of soft cedar and redwood. A club used to stun sea lions would be shaped, smoothed, carved, and polished till it suggested a royal scepter more than an instrument for cracking skulls. Spoons were so elaborately designed that they appeared ready to fly, swim or run away, or even to bite the user's hand. Wooden spoons the size of soup ladles were studded with bird wings, raven beaks, salmon fins, bear paws, and beaver teeth.

Stone adzes were always to be heard chipping away at wood, dogfish skin rasping at it in the manner of sandpaper. From spoons, paddles, and clubs, it was natural that the carvers should turn to the lodge itself. Rafters, corner poles, and entire walls became a menagerie of carved ravens, beavers, halibut, and bears—figures that told the history of the people within the lodge and attested to the rank of its chief.

This urge to advertise was responsible for the totem pole. In the time between salmon runs, carvers would chip away patiently at twenty-foot logs to produce a vertical chain of heraldic crests and figures. These were not static symbols. Eyes bulged and mouths gaped in wide, toothy grins. Pigments from charcoal, berries, cinnabar, and salmon eggs were brilliantly applied in bold, swirling lines of blue, white, and yellow that diverged and converged in tigerlike symmetry to outline a face.

Lacking any mechanism such as a crane for lifting, the men would dig a pit six feet deep at the base of a totem pole, and hollow out the backside so as to lighten it. The tip would be gradually propped up, with men pulling on a rope attached to it and strung over a high prop until they had eased the totem into its pit.

Once erect, such poles would last between sixty and seventy years. Their height as well as the quality of the carving was a matter of prestige. A man might raise a totem to ridicule a competitor or a debtor, showing the target of ridicule with a downcast face. The totems and the richly carved lodges of the Northwest Pacific may be said to have anticipated the neon signs of Las Vegas. Yet they had a graceful power that is lacking in their gaudy commercial descendants.

The carving of totems was not much practiced south of Puget Sound. Among the tribes to the south, the preferred symbols of wealth included certain mollusks. Among the Yurok it was the dentalium, a mollusk with a delicate, curving, toothlike shell four inches long, which they used as a form of currency and eagerly hoarded. How did the Yurok get such quantities of a shell that normally is found in fairly deep water? Beds of dentalium do flourish at moderate depths off Vancouver Island, where the whale-chasing Nootka Indians had developed a way to harvest them. They would thrust a huge broom of wood splints into the dentalium beds, then compress the splints with a heavy, sliding board, and finally retrieve the splints with the shells trapped between. How did the Nootka keep track of where the beds were in those unmarked waters? They triangulated the location with two natural features on shore, such as mountain peaks. Outsiders were never privy to the device they used. The shell was traded southward, tribe by tribe, increasing in value all the while until it reached the Yurok—for whom a single fine specimen could be enough to buy a bride. It was these tiny mollusks that brought the Nootka the wealth to commission bigger and better totems.

Dancing, especially during the long, rainy winters in the lodges, was another means of expression. Dancers who weren't glorifying a chief's heritage might try to scare the wits out of their audience. Wood-carvers supplied gaudy and gruesome monster masks; and in the dance, heads were continually being severed, hearts pierced, arms bitten off. This may sound ferocious and "savage"—but think how we ourselves revel in Dracula and Frankenstein. To mimic a stabbing, dancers would press down on seal bladders filled with animal blood. A woman dancer might be placed on a table to be beheaded, and a male dancer might go prancing about the lodge with a bloody head. A trap door would enable the woman to exit and leave a head mask behind. Drums and rattles made things scarier. Fires would be stoked with kelp bulbs that popped like firecrackers. Some dancers sprinkled their well-greased bodies with goldlike mica that flickered in the shadowy firelight of the lodge.

Indians interviewed by anthropologists have attested to the haunting effect of these dances. A husband once saw his dancing wife tied up, carted out of the lodge, paddled off in a canoe, and thrown overboard. Sobbing uncontrollably by this time, the poor fellow didn't know that the dancers had substituted for his wife a young man who, after being thrown overboard, had been quickly retrieved on the far side of the canoe, hidden from the view of those onshore.

These dances were not impromptu, but were staged by choreographers who, like the carvers, were hired by chiefs, and rehearsed their casts in the seclusion of the nearest forest.

Totem poles and dancing were often integrated into a ceremonial potlatch, a party that was the ultimate in prestige-making. Potlatches were given for such special events as a marriage, a birth, or the accession of an heir to the rank of chief. However, the central purpose was always a display of rank; this would establish the right of an heir to his new position. One anthropologist, Philip Drucker, has compared the procedure to notarizing a document or registering a deed. Besides unveiling a new totem pole or dance to commemorate his origins, the host would display his wealth simply by giving it away. Feasts were one means of doing so. An abundance of berries, halibut, candlefish oil, salmon, fern roots, and so on, would become a trial of the guests' internal fortitude. They didn't so much as have to lift a finger to be fed; the food was put in their mouths by the anxious hosts. The guests would be told where the berries and salmon had been harvested, so as to validate a chief's claim to the territory. Gifts of otter pelts, bear robes, and even canoes were also made, each one carefully graded to suit the rank of a particular guest.

Thorstein Veblen would have seen his *Theory of the Leisure Class* confirmed in the cedar lodges of the Pacific coast Indians. Just as for the inland tribes the scarcity of resources often led to war, the sheer abundance along the Pacific shore made gift-giving and display a social necessity. The potlatch, the totem poles, the wind-felled cedars, the winter dances, the salmon snares, the plank canoes, the stunning basketry, the sage-bark diapers, the abalone-shell earrings, all reflected the natural richness of the Pacific shore. Eventually all of these responses were to undergo a transformation that was almost suicidal.

Chapter 3

Natives and Newcomers Collide

The appraisal of Geronimo Boscana, who served as a Franciscan missionary to the California coastal Indians from 1806 to 1831, was typical:

> No doubt these Indians passed a miserable life, ever idle, and more like the brutes than rational beings. They neither cultivated the ground, nor planted any kind of grain; but lived upon the wild seeds of the field, the fruits of the forest, and upon the abundance of game. It is really surprising, that during the lapse of many ages, with their reason and experience, they had not advanced one iota in improving the things that would have been useful and convenient for them; for instance, in agriculture; in planting and cultivating those seeds which were most appreciated; also trees around their dwellings, bearing such fruit as they were obliged to bring from a great distance. But no! Nothing of the kind! And in no part of the province was to be found aught but the common, spontaneous productions of the earth.

A Chinook story, recorded in Ella Clark's *Indian Legends of the Pacific Northwest,* suggests that the original inhabitants were equally unimpressed by the newcomers to their region:

> As she [a Chinook woman] returned to the village, she saw a strange something out in the water not far from shore. At first she thought it was a whale. When she came nearer, she saw two spruce trees standing upright on it.
>
> "It is not a whale," she said to herself. "It is a monster."

When she came nearer the strange thing that lay at the edge of the water, she saw that its outside was covered with copper and that ropes were tied to the spruce trees. Then a bear came out of the strange thing and stood on it. He looked like a bear, but his face was the face of a human being.

A culture based entirely on natural values came into collision with one that had little esteem for those values. The early explorers could appreciate the seaworthiness of plank and dugout canoes, particularly after the effort of hiking up and down a three-thousand-foot coastal range.

But they had great difficulty in appreciating such other aspects of this coastal culture as its food gathering habits. How could any civilized people simply go around with stick in hand to dig up "the common, spontaneous productions of the earth?" Otto von Kotzebue, who explored the Pacific coast for the Russian government in the early nineteenth century observed: "They are not difficult in the choice of their food, but consume the most disgusting things, not exceeding all kinds of worms and insects, with good appetite, only avoiding poisonous snakes." According to another observer, "Their dinner is a fast." Soon the explorers were calling these coastal people "digger Indians." The simplicity of their life, their near-nakedness and houses of matted reeds were taken as signs of a backward state. Only those who wore black robes or leather jerkins, even in that mild

Mediterranean climate, could be considered civilized. For the newcomers, the smell of the body grease that protected the Indians from sunburn and frostbite became a personal affront. Added to the smoke, the heat, and the oily fish odors inside the cedar lodges, affront became an olfactory outrage.

People who avoided raising a sweat by working too hard were suspect as cultural delinquents. Those who built houses to raise a sweat for pleasure, as the California Indians did in their *temescals,* all but invited damnation. That these people, despite their seemingly backward technology, found leisure for folk arts and entertainment became another indictment. As Boscana wrote, "They passed their time in plays, and roaming about from house to house, dancing and sleeping; and this was their only occupation, and the mode of life most common amongst them from day to day."

Still more exasperating was the potential wealth that was being frittered away in games and dancing. Explorers exhausted by landing in the surf and climbing the bluff would gaze admiringly at an Indian with ninety pounds of merchandise on his back, able to cross the coastal range and withstand brisk temperatures in his greasy state of undress, even as he slept beneath a pine tree. But this weatherproof human machine preferred dancing to a life of moving, carrying, digging, chopping and hunting ten hours a day, six days a week—a most perplexing vice to men who regarded *Work* as a virtue in itself.

The tribulations of early explorers and settlers did not help them to appreciate the coastal Indians. For those newly arrived in the wilderness, life was often a struggle for control over their nerves and digestive functions. Starved after a long sea voyage or an overland expedition, the explorers would eagerly devour the salmon proffered by coastal Indians—and then pay unexpected consequences. According to John Townsend, a young ornithologist with the Wyeth expedition that reached the Columbia watershed in 1834, "The sudden and entire change from flesh exclusively, to fish, has affected us all, more or less, with diarrhea and pain in the abdomen; several of the men have been so extremely sick, as scarcely to be able to travel."

The North Pacific coast Indians, with their inverted basket hats and winter lodge dances, did not mind their rainy winter wilderness. To early explorers, its wetness only confirmed their views of nature. After traversing the dry lands of eastern Oregon, the Lewis and Clark expedition found the green coastal terrain "as grateful to the eye as it is useful in supplying us with fuel." But there followed a four-month winter stay at Fort Clatsop on the Oregon coast, during which there were only twelve days without rain and six without clouds. The lushness of the coastal forests often limited visibility to a hundred yards for eager elk hunters. After climbing over fallen timbers and stumbling through coastal bogs, the exhausted hunters might have to stay overnight in the dank forests. "Rained all the last night. We covered ourselves as well as we could with elk skin, and sat up the greater part of the night all wet. I lay in the wet verry cold," Clark reported of one such occasion. In early spring, when the huckleberries were coming into leaf, the members of the expedition gladly turned their backs on the coastal forest. Now, according to Lewis, the sight of treeless plains was "particularly pleasing after having been so long imprisoned in mountains and those almost impenetrably thick forests of the sea coast."

The early explorers did express some tender feelings in the midst of the wilderness. A British captain, Charles Bishop, wrote of the Chinook Indians on the Columbia, "They delighted in feeding us well and were disappointed if we did not eat heartily. They fed our dogs, too." John Boit, a seaman who visited the North Pacific coast with American Captain Robert Gray in 1791, observed: "The Women are very pretty. They are akin a state of nature, except the females, who wear a leaf apron (perhaps 'twas a fig leaf). But some of our gentlemen, that examin'd them pretty close and *near,* both *within* and *without* reported that it was not a leaf but a nice wove mat in resemblance!!"

But these encounters were not always mutually beneficial. After reaching the Oregon coast in November of 1805, Clark reported:

An old woman & wife to a cheif of the *Chunnooks* came and made a Camp near ours. She brought with her 6 young Squars (*her daughters & nieces*) I believe for the purpose of Gratifying the passions of the men of our party and receiving for these indulgiences Such small presents as She (the old woman) thought proper to accept of.

Those people appear to View Sensuality as a Necessary evel, and do not appear to abhor it as a Crime in the unmarried State. The young females are fond of the attention of our men and appear to meet the sincere approbation of their friends and connections, for thus obtaining their favors . . . I saw on the left arm of a Squar the following letters *J. Bowman.*

By the time this same Indian party revisited the expedition in Fort Clatsop, Lewis reported a matter that had intervened to impede their relations with his men: "We were visited this afternoon by . . . a Chinnook Chief his wife and six women of his nation which the old baud had brought for market. This was the same party that had communicated the venerial to so many of our party in November last, and of which they have finally recovered. I therefore gave the men a particular charge with rispect to them which they promised me to observe."

The coastal Indians of California aroused the overweaning pity of Spanish missionaries, who enticed and cajoled them into converting to Christianity. The happy Chumash Indians of the islands off the coast of Santa Barbara were inclined to resist such recruitment. Rebuffed, the missionaries found an ally in the natural environment when in 1812 an earthquake struck the Santa Barbara area. On Santa Rosa Island a crack measuring a thousand yards long, over a hundred feet wide and as much as sixty feet deep, opened up. In the Santa Barbara Channel the earthquake churned up seismic waves that battered the uplands along the shore. In the wake of this disaster, the Indians' homeland became a nightmare. In 1884, H. W. Henshaw of the Smithsonian Institution wrote of interviewing a survivor:

The waters receded from the island several hundred yards. This so alarmed the Indians that, fearful that the island was about to be engulfed, they departed and were settled in bands of three or four hundred at the several missions. The above is the story told by the Indian (Anisetto Tajilacheet). It is not difficult to read the power of the priests in this abandonment. Doubtless prediction of heavy punishment in case the islanders still proved contumacious had often been made by the priests, and this earthquake was interpreted by the superstitious Indians as the first of a series of fatal catastrophes.

The Indians exchanged paddles for hoes, shifted to a diet of red meat and grain and were assigned a single language. To have transformed them from seagoing food gatherers to perspiring farm workers, however justifiable it seemed to the Spanish friars, amounted to "saving souls only at the inevitable cost of lives," in the words of the anthropologist A. L. Kroeber. The short life span at these missions was less the result of inhumane treatment than of the Indians' lack of immunity to the common cold, which often developed into tuberculosis or pneumonia. Indians afflicted with such new diseases as measles or mumps would flee for relief to the sweathouse, and the ensuing dash into the cold water of a river or the ocean would have fatal consequences. When the mission system disintegrated, the coastal Indians were left without resources. The abalone was still on the shore and the acorns still lay on the ground, but the mission Indians, estranged from their original environment, now required supervision to keep alive even as farm hands. Unemployment, epidemics, homicide, and drink thinned their ranks. The arrival of Anglo-Saxon settlers in California only worsened their plight. As Professor Sherbourne Cook of the University of California at Berkeley has observed, although Ibero–Americans exploited the Indian, they wanted to keep him alive and tolerated intermarriage. The Anglo-Americans wanted only his land, not his labor. They could afford to kill him off. Some coastal Indians finally became familiar with scalping . . . at the hands of self-appointed Indian fighters.

Because the Spanish were not attracted very far

beyond the coastal ranges, the Indian tribes of the interior were generally left alone. While the coastal Indians were being divested of their culture, the interior Indians began to resist the occasional forays of the Spanish. While coastal Indians were learning to toll mission bells, those of the interior learned to ride horses and shoot rifles. They resisted so fiercely and valiantly that many were accorded the dubious honor of having reservations set aside for them. The coastal Indians died out, shorn of their ability to survive, much less resist. It was their demise that brought the attention of the public in America to the need for a reservation system. The California coastal Indians, with their dense populations and maritime abundance, became the victims of a culture at odds with their own. "It was one of the last human hunts of civilization and the worst and most brutal of them all," wrote the historian Hubert Howe Bancroft. Occasionally, erosion or a bulldozer cutting through for a new road will turn up an abalone earring, a deerbone flute or soapstone carving—the frail remnant of a vanished culture that once expressed much joy in living.

Since unlike the sunny coastal plains of southern California, the forests along the North Pacific coast did not encourage immediate settlement, the Indians there were given a temporary reprieve. Like those of the California interior, many of them learned to resist, only to be outflanked by their native habitat. Those of Puget Sound who laid siege to the budding community of Seattle were routed, not by cavalry but by three U.S. naval warships. When another of those warships drew up alongside an Indian village in southern Alaska, the natives retreated into the forests. Navy guns proceeded to level the houses, and a party went ashore to destroy all the canoes, reducing the once self-reliant Indians to forlorn candidates for reservation life.

On the inland reservations to which coastal groups were transplanted, an Indian who had been able to keep his family in food for months by a week of salmon fishing now found that he had to plow, weed and plant the year round to subsist, rainfall permitting. All too often, the reservation system converted a self-reliant individual into a frustrated welfare recipient.

Those coastal Indians who managed to stay in their traditional habitat fared better. But some became the victims of their own prosperity. Indians who had originally harvested marine mammals for food and clothing now slaughtered them in return for iron knives, blankets, watches, costume jewelry and liquor offered by fur traders. The massacres of fur seals now brought in iron tools to be used in chiseling larger and more intricate totem poles. As fur seals became scarce, another bonanza took their place: salvaging shipwrecks along the treacherous coast. Crockery from London, gowns from New York, and quantities of whiskey washed ashore, along with so many corpses that existing cemeteries were soon swamped. Men who had once sung in praise of whales and of the first salmon now gave homage to a new kind of prosperity:

> What do you think I live for?
> I live to drink whiskey.
> Have pity on me,
>   foam children.*

Seal massacres and salvage sprees now meant bigger potlatches. Their tempo became feverish. A Kwakiutl Indian, Daniel Cranmer, described a 1921 potlatch to an anthropologist, Helen Codere:

> The second day a xwexwe dance with the shells was given to me by the chief of Cape Mudge. I gave him a gas boat and fifty dollars cash. Altogether that was worth five hundred dollars. I paid him back double. He also gave some names. The same day I gave Hudson's Bay blankets. I started giving out the property, first the canoes. Two pool tables were given to two chiefs . . . The pool tables were worth three hundred and fifty dollars apiece. Then bracelets, gaslights, violins, guitars were given to the more important people. Then twenty-four canoes, some of them big ones, and four gas boats . . .
>
> Then I gave button blankets, shawls and common blankets. There were four hundred of the real, old Hudson's Bay blankets. I gave these away with the xwexwe dances. I also gave lots of small change with the Hudson's Bay blankets. I threw it away for the

* Songs of the Tlingit as recorded by John R. Swanton.

45

kids to get. There were also basins, maybe a thousand of them, glasses, washtubs, teapots and cups given to the women in order of their positions.

The third day I don't remember what happened.

The fourth day I gave furniture: boxes, trunks, sewing machines, gramophones, bedsteads and bureaus.

The fifth day I gave away cash.

The sixth day I gave away about a thousand sacks of flour worth three dollars a sack. I also gave sugar.

Everyone admits that this was the biggest yet. I am proud to say our people are ahead . . . So I am a big man in those days. Nothing new. In the old days this was my weapon and I could call down anyone. All the chiefs say now in a gathering, "You cannot expect that we can ever get up to you. You are a great mountain."

Sometimes measles and other epidemics brought by white men would sweep through Indian villages. A visitor to one Chinook village reported, "There were fires smoking, dogs barking, salmon drying on the racks. Only one thing was lacking, the cheerful sound of the human voice." Such widespread mortalities brought confusion to the hierarchy of rank. Claimants might try to outdo each other in what were called rival potlatches. In 1895, a potlatch planner exhorted the Kwakiutl Indians of Fort Rupert:

> Friends, I ask you to keep yourselves in readiness, for the Koskimo are like to a vast mountain of wealth, from which rocks are rolling down all the time. If we do not defend ourselves we shall be buried by their property. Behold, friends! They are dancing and making merry day after day. But we are not doing so. Remember, this is our village and our battlefield. If we do not open our eyes and awake, we shall lose our high rank. Remember, Kwakiutl, we have never been vanquished by another tribe.

Sometimes canoes were hacked apart, and oil poured on the fire until the lodge roofs were ablaze —an act of planned destruction showing that the potlatch giver could afford to destroy his own wealth. What had been a rather gracious distribution of natural wealth had degenerated into a feverish exercise in conspicuous consumption.

As the populations of sea otter, halibut, and salmon were depleted, the means for holding potlatches vanished. The Depression of the thirties was the final blow. Reservation authorities frowned on the wastefulness of potlatches and proceeded to ban them, even when they were still a genuine means of holding the community together. An agent for the Makah group on Cape Flattery was relieved that "his" Indians willingly gave up potlatches in favor of Christmas and other Christian holidays. When he saw his charges celebrating one another's birthdays, he was pleased by their civilized progress. The Indians were likewise happy to see their agent so pleased. They had simply gone on giving potlatches under the guise of Christmas and birthday gift-giving.

Reservation life tended to wear down such cultural resistance, however. Sometimes Indians helped to destroy their own culture. European museum directors who, willing to pay hundreds of dollars for totem poles, made the journey to a coastal village would arrive to find poles chopped down and hacked up for firewood, the Indians having concluded that the ancestral carvings only advertised their cultural backwardness. Newly acquired Christian morality inspired one Indian to shoot a penis off one totem pole.

Today, the North Pacific coast Indians carry on a rather unstable existence on their reservation lands, dependent to a great degree on the whims of resource politics and an industrial economy. Totem poles and scare masks are back in fashion now that tourists go looking for them. And the Indians find themselves bound by the fish and game restrictions that have been made necessary by industrial pollution and the voracious demands of an assembly-line economy. This notion of asking them to share the burden of conservation has become the perennial rationale for breaking treaties that originally ensured Indians access to resources on which they have traditionally depended for a living.

Ironically, as the remnants of the native culture are shunted about in courtrooms, legislative chambers, and the offices of canning companies, its merits are finally being appreciated. Some early visitors to the Pacific shore attempted to appreciate the Indian on his own terms rather than on preconceived standards of the visitor. Pedro Font recorded this observation of a fellow Franciscan missionary in California in 1775:

Father Garces is so well-equipped to live with the Indians and fraternize with them, that he himself often appears to be one. In all difficulties he is as impassive as the Indians. He sits in the circle with them, or by the fire at night, with his legs crossed; and will meditate quietly for many hours, ignoring everything else, talking serenely and calmly to them. Although the Indian foods are as disgusting and dirty as these strange people themselves, the Father eats them with fine appetite and claims that they are tasty and healthful to the stomach.

Font saw this empathy as something to be exploited. "Briefly, it seems to me that God has created him [Father Garces] precisely as an instrument of relationship with these miserable, ignorant, and outlandish nations."

During the late eighteenth and early nineteenth centuries, a small group of dedicated anthropologists and ethnologists eagerly sought out, observed, interviewed, and lived among these coastal Indians for whom forests, the supply of salmon, and an entire way of life were ebbing away. There were still many Indian groups to study on the north Pacific coast, but in southern California the last of the full-blooded Chumash were dying out, and the anthropologists had to settle for combing through refuse heaps and the sketchy accounts of Spanish explorers. Thanks to the tireless work of these men, we now realize how tragically the culture of these coastal people has been underestimated. The Indians, seemingly so ill-clad, so poorly fed, sheltered, and equipped, were actually, in the words of one anthropologist, "born naturalists, familiar from earliest childhood with the animals and plants of the regions in which they live. It is not strange, therefore, that their occupations and beliefs; in fact, their entire lives and thoughts; center about natural objects." So wrote Dr. C. D. Merriam, whose search for surviving Indians took him along unnumbered canyons and wilderness watersheds in California. A California newspaper article asserting that Indians showed "almost no faculty of invention or imagination . . . Except in that limited area of their minds that was developed by their primitive environment, their mentality is that of morons," led him to protest:

Can anyone examine the beautifully wrought canoes of the Klamath River Indians, dug out of the trunks of huge trees by means of elkhorn chisels, and perfectly adapted for navigation in a river in bars, rapids, and whirlpools; or can anyone look at the graceful and pleasing forms of their delicately woven baskets ornamented by intricate and beautiful designs; or at their aboriginal aprons, fashioned so elegantly of plant fibers and decorated with a multitude of carefully braided pendants in contrasting colors, beautified by the addition at regular intervals of shells, pine nuts, and other articles; can anyone behold such objects as these without realizing not only the perfect adaption of the materials at hand to the needs of the household, but also a well developed appreciation of art and love of the beautiful. Is this in harmony with "the mentality of morons"?

As the culture that produced such objects ebbed away the newcomers as well as the Indians became the poorer. "It may be overtaxing the truth to say that we have as much to learn from them as they from us," Merriam wrote, "but nevertheless, and entirely apart from their superior knowledge of the food, textile, and medicinal values of animals and plants, they can put us to shame in matters of patience, fairness, honor, and kindness."

How different the outcome might have been if this knowledge and appreciation of the natural environment had been preserved rather than condemned! Certainly such knowledge would be useful to us today as we attempt to redeem some of the natural values that have been so carelessly squandered. As marine biologists sift through shell middens to discover the original biological makeup of the fast-vanishing estuarine areas in southern California, the knowledge they gain may help in restoring these areas if and when their importance is recognized.

To preserve such midden sites for future study, archeologists use aerial surveys and infrared photography. But the safety even of sites already discovered is not always assured. According to Roger

DeSautels of the Archeological Research Institute in Costa Mesa, California, in fifty years only one judicial sentence has been pronounced as a result of charges under the Antiquities Act, ostensibly passed to protect the nation's archeological heritage. DeSautels, despite such setbacks as the nuclear tests on Amchitka, has higher hopes for the National Environmental Policy Act, which contains a reference to "irreplaceable resources" that may apply to the protection and salvage of middens. "After all," he points out, "we can't get the Indians to come back and live on the land again."

No quantity of infrared cameras and environmental impact statements will be able to retrieve myths, songs, and folklore that have gone unrecorded. Archeologists looking at the beautiful, semiabstract cave paintings left by the Chumash can do little more than refer to them as "ceremonial"—their refuge in the face of the unknown.

Such collaboration as the work of fishery scientists with Indians of the Lummi reservation on Puget Sound in salmon and oyster culture programs, although too late for the coastal Indians of southern California, may help those of the North Pacific coast to develop a modern version of their once-flourishing culture. With technical aid from the Oceanic Foundation in Hawaii, the Lummi have grown some twenty million oysters and over five million trout and salmon fingerlings in diked tidelands. Some of the fingerlings will be used to restore salmon runs. Lummi who have carried on a marginal existence as lumbermen, factory workers, and bead stringers are returning to the reservation where the tidelands their forefathers once harvested as hunters are now being farmed by the new methods. Yet their future remains uncertain as challenges to even a partial reliance on natural values continue to emerge. One of these is a terminal complex for storing and refining Alaskan crude oil, recently established as a neighbor of the reservation, which brings with it the threat of pollution.

In 1851, while visiting the Yurok of Trinidad Bay in northern California, Carl Meyer observed:

> Sometimes when I was in the presence of a group of Allequas, lost in the contemplation of the conditions peculiar to the mode of life of these naked men, which from a superficial point of view afford so much occasion for pity, I would suddenly be surprised by a derisive laugh, and the group would disperse as though shamed or insulted at being pitied by a white. "Don't weep about us, weep about yourself," seems to be the native's answer to the sympathy of the white and I cannot blame them for this.

Chapter 4

The Big Bonanza

In 1835 a sailor aboard an American trading vessel, the *Alert,* docked in San Francisco Bay, observed nearby a shipload of Alaskan Indians transported there by Russians to hunt seals and handle shipments of tallow. The sailor was Henry Dana, and he later wrote, in *Two Years Before the Mast:*

> They had brutish faces, looked like the antipodes of sailors, and apparently dealt in nothing but grease. They lived upon grease; ate it, drank it, slept in the midst of it, and their clothes were covered with it. To the Russian [Alaskan], grease is the greatest luxury. They looked with greedy eyes upon the tallow-bags as they were taken into the vessel, and, no doubt, would have eaten one up whole, had not the officer kept watch over it. The grease appeared to fill their pores, and to come out in their hair and on their faces. It seems as if it were this saturation which makes them stand cold and rain so well. If they were to go into a warm climate, they would melt and die of the scurvy.

Such fixations would recur again and again, up and down the Pacific shore. While the minds and energies of the coastal Indians were attuned to every aspect of their environment, the newcomers would focus theirs on a particular aspect to be exploited—tallow, lumber, oil, or salmon. Exploitation became the whole of their existence.

And such fixations were not easily deterred. California first appeared on maps as an island close to China. The monarchs of Spain were eager to find a shortcut to Cathay, and Nature was expected to oblige. After it had been shown as an island in some hundred maps, King Ferdinand VII of Spain in 1747 was obliged to decree: "California is not an island." This was the first but not the last time that the Pacific shore was to fail the Spanish. When there were no more reserves of Aztec gold and silver to plunder, the Spanish turned anxiously toward Alta California. To reach this possible source of new riches, early Spanish explorers sailed out of Acapulco, Mexico, and up the Baja California peninsula, bucking headwinds for seven hundred miles. Juan Rodriguez Cabrillo, the discoverer of California, was nine months reaching what is now San Diego. Fog awaited these men, along with more headwinds, as they moved up the coast. Reversing direction at Cape Mendocino, so that he had the cursed winds at his back, Cabrillo had hoped for more leisurely exploration. By this time, however, his men had energy left for but one goal: getting back to Acapulco. Their gums swollen with scurvy, they could hardly chew or swallow their food. Sometimes they were too weak to climb the mast and tend the sails. For lack of energy, there would be prolonged debate over whether to cut loose an anchor or haul it in. On that journey Cabrillo himself never made it back to Acapulco. He died on San Miguel Island in 1542, apparently from aftereffects of a broken arm. On an expedition in 1602–1603, Sebastián Vizcaíno lost forty-two men.

Despite scurvy, headwinds, fog, and the menacing mountain coast, the mere hint of silver or gold continued to inflame the minds of Spaniards. One Father Ascensión, traveling with Vizcaíno, observed in San Diego, "In the sand on this beach there is a great quantity of yellow pyrites, all full of holes, a sure sign that in the neighboring mountains and adjacent to this port there are gold mines." Father Ascensión also saw local Indians handling some stones "which glistened like silver ribbons. These stones seemed to be of rich silver ore . . ." There was indeed gold in California, but the Spanish were never to find it. They stayed near the coast; the gold was in the Sierras.

The Spanish settled for a more modest prize: a usable port, which would provide for Philippine galleons en route to Acapulco a respite from scurvy and from ambushes in the fog by Drake and other English privateers. The Spanish had no way of knowing that there were only three prime natural harbors on the Pacific shore. The entrance to the best one, San Francisco Bay, was so unpromising in its shroud of fog that naval explorers passed it by. Vizcaíno, determined to will a port into being, described what he found:

> It is all that can be desired for commodiousness and as a station for ships making the voyage to the Philippines, sailing whence they make a landfall on this coast. This port is sheltered from all winds, while on the immediate coast there are pines from which masts of any desired size can be obtained, as well as live oaks and white oaks, rosemary, rock roses, the rose of Alexandria, a great variety of game, such as rabbits, hares, partridges, and other sorts and species found in Spain and in greater abundance than in the Sierra Morena . . . As some port or place on this coast is to be occupied, none is so proper for the purpose as this harbor of Monterey.

A century and a half later, the Portolá expedition was dispatched overland to occupy Vizcaíno's port and to ward off the Russians. Finding it now became a challenge. According to one member of the overland expedition, Miguel Costanzó:

> We did not know what to think of the situation. A port so famous as that of Monterey, so celebrated, and so talked of in its time, by energetic, skillful and intelligent men, expert sailors who came expressly to reconnoiter these coasts, by order of the monarch who at that time governed the Spains—is it possible to say that it has not been found after the most careful and earnest efforts, carried out at the cost of much toil and fatigue? Or, is it admissible to think that it has been filled up, or destroyed in the course of time?

Another member, Father Juan Crespi, wondered "if the port of Monterey had been hidden in some corner." While looking for the elusive bay, the expedition stumbled across another bay so large "not only all the navy of our most Catholic majesty, but those of all Europe could take shelter in it," as Crespi reported. Since the port of Monterey had not been found, however, the expedition had to pass up what would one day be known as San Francisco Bay. When the object of their quest was finally discovered, the reason for its elusiveness became apparent. The bay in reality is not fully protected from winds; Vizcaíno had so overpraised its potentialities that later explorers had difficulty in recognizing it. But orders were orders. Monterey, not San Francisco, became the Spanish capital of Alta California.

Since Alta California did not live up to royal expectations, the interest of the Spanish crown declined. The resident Spanish population never rose much above four thousand. The climate and the coastal landscape were very similar to those at home, but that wasn't what the Spanish were after.

Notwithstanding their small numbers, the residents despoiled one native resource: the coastal Indians who were recruited to fulfill the need of the Spanish crown for agricultural labor and the need of the mission system for souls to save.

Other native resources were little used. Redwoods were cut occasionally and their trunks sawed into cartwheels. For shelter, the Spanish relied on adobe more than on wood. And they imported their own economy—raising cattle on ranchos.

Despite this rather modest enterprise, there were some interesting premonitions of the future. In 1830, government officials put into effect a pioneer regulation on tree cutting: "No large piece of wood shall be destroyed in order to obtain a small piece, that is, there shall be no wanton waste." Three years later, Governor José Figueroa, having "learned that certain trees, which had been planted on the side of the road and formed a part of the beautiful Alameda extending from Santa Clara to San Jose, were being cut down for firewood . . . ordered the vandalism to cease immediately, and took measures that nothing of the kind should be attempted for the future."

Ironically, the rule of Spain and that of Mexico, which succeeded it, could only be characterized by a term the Spanish had applied to the coastal Indians: indolent. As one American visitor noted, the Spanish "did nothing that couldn't be done from the back of a horse." Another foreign visitor said that playing cards were the only reading matter known to the residents. Visitors from Britain, France, and England, as they appraised the Pacific coast, saw the possibility of one bonanza after another—lumber in the forest, pelts in the seal rookeries, and salmon in the rivers. In a land that lay waiting for the ax, the fish net, and the rifle, the Spanish raised cattle and cut the redwoods for cartwheels. In the 1840s, Duflot de Mofras told his French sponsors in a confidential memo ("The Easy Conquest of California") that the Pacific coast could provide enough wood to reduce the country's costly dependence on Norwegian wood, with enough left over to floor, wall and roof all the islands in the Pacific.

But it was a young and growing nation, rather than the great powers, that would supplant the pastoral rancho era as new opportunity opened. In 1848, the Pacific had one of the last virgin shores left in the northern hemisphere. A century and a half later, this virgin shore would have become one of the most highly developed and also one of the most abused. By the mid-nineteenth century, the industrial age was coming into its own. As technology and demand depleted the forests of Maine and the midwest and the fisheries of New England, the Pacific coast offered the biggest and most varied bonanza of all. There would be little time for it to be known as a homeland or as a birthplace. There were no memories to be cherished, only expectations to be fulfilled. The Pacific coast had let the Spanish down; the new migrants would not allow that to happen to them.

From across the continent the poet Walt Whitman considered this mobilization of human enterprise and wrote his "Song of the Redwood-Tree." For him, "the crash, the muffled shriek, the groan" of severed redwoods was not a hymn of death, but a paean to the future.

The new society at last, proportionate to Nature,
In man of you, more than your mountain peaks or
    stalwart trees imperial,
In woman more, far more, than all your gold or
    vines, or even vital air.

Fresh come, to a new world indeed, yet long prepared,
I see the genius of the modern, child of the real
    and ideal,
Clearing the ground for broad humanity, the true
    America, heir of the past so grand,
To build a grander future.

The pelt of the sea otter that frolicked in the kelp forests—smooth, jet-black with an underlay of silvery hairs—singled it out as the first victim in a series of Pacific coast bonanzas. It began in 1778 when Captain James Cook and his men reached the Pacific Northwest and replaced their worn-out clothes by trading glass beads with the Indians for otter pelts. Subsequently, Cook's seamen found that the Chinese would pay handsomely for these pelts. The vessels of British, French, American, and Russian fur traders converged along the North Pacific, often accompanied by undercover military agents intent on surveying the Spanish presidios farther down coast. As arrows, harpoons, clubs, and powder balls hailed down on the sea otters, their natural defenses became obsolete or suicidal. One hunter, Captain John Meares, noted that "parental affection supersedes all sense of danger, and both the male and female defend their offspring with the most furious courage, tearing out the arrows and harpoons fixed in them with their teeth and oftentimes even attacking the canoes." In 1801–1802, some 15,000 otter skins were traded for silk, tea, and cotton cloth. As more and more vessels swept down the coast, the once-teeming rookeries were dying out, particularly around the Channel Islands.

In the Pacific Northwest, Indians did the killing and skinning. The California Indians who were not yet living in missions were not considered diligent enough as hunters. Glass beads and iron nails were not a sufficient inducement. Undeterred, the Russians brought in Aleuts from Alaska whom they described as "Cossacks of the North Pacific," to hunt out the Channel Island otters.

Cook and his men had run short of clothes in 1778. By 1822, the otter fur trade was already in decline. There was indeed one limit to this bonanza: the virtual demise of the otters. Were there traps, were there pitfalls on the way to Whitman's "grander future"? Undeterred, the traders ransacked the Pacific coast for other means to wealth. The mandarins of China used seal bristles as pipe cleaners and their sex organs as charms. Seal oil was needed for lamps. In the slaughter of elephant seals that ensued, they both became as scarce as otters. Islands once teeming with squealing otter and seal rookeries were left to the seabirds.

To keep the bonanza from running out, traders turned to the ranchos for hides and tallow. The carcasses of cattle slaughtered only for their skins soon dotted the California landscape, a bonanza for vultures and condors.

Another source of oil and of wealth was discovered offshore: the gray whale that migrated between summer feeding grounds in the Chukchi Sea and its winter calving grounds in the lagoons of Baja California. The ceremonial harpooning expeditions of the Nootka Indians were superseded by an effort at assembly-line destruction. Coastal whaling stations sprang up to ambush the gray whale. The trade in whalebone helped pave the sidewalks of Monterey. At first it appeared that the gray whales did not congregate in slaughter-prone rookeries as the otters and sea elephants had done. But in 1857 Captain Charles Scammon, commanding the whaler *Boston*, cruised out of San Francisco into a winter calving lagoon midway along the coast of lower California. A year later, a whaling fleet followed Scammon to the lagoon. Harpooned whales plunged in every direction, entangling lines, colliding with boats and with one another. There were curses in a variety of languages as the tangled

lines were cut, and competing boat crews exchanged continual threats. Four years later, Scammon Lagoon had yielded 22,230 barrels of oil, and gray whaling was no longer economical. Years later, Scammon revisited the lagoon as he gathered information for *The Marine Mammals of the Northwestern Coast of North America.* "The decayed carcasses and bleaching bones strewed along the shores," he wrote, "gave evidence of the havoc made by the most enterprising and energetic class of seamen that sailed under our national flag." But Scammon had his doubts about this enterprise. "Ere long, may it not be that the California gray will be known only as an extinct species of Pacific cetaceans?"

By the 1850s, entrepreneurs had found a new source of wealth. A lumberman had to go into the woods, a sealer to the rookeries; but for an entrepreneur who set up a salmon cannery at a river mouth, the fish would swim straight to it. Huge salmon nets, strung across the river mouth, were dragged by horses along the river banks. Salmon began piling up at the cannery. Hired Indians didn't work fast enough; Chinese immigrants brought in to build railroads across the Sierra were transported to Oregon and Washington to speed up cannery operations and thwart unionization. Even they weren't fast enough. A machine that could gut and slice the salmon was devised. It was called the Iron Chink. Now, the horses had to work faster. Some would be caught and drowned by tidal currents. Power boats began to replace them.

Fights to corner the salmon supply were inevitable. "Corking" a net—that is, setting it in front of your competitor's—was too complicated for some people, who merely cut the competitor's net. Some entrepreneurs were able to corner a salmon run by occupying all the land around the river mouth. Their defeated competitors began wondering, why not turn a ship into a cannery and anchor it off a river mouth? Salmon were now confronted with nets strung by an offshore as well as an onshore cannery operator. Things had changed radically since the days of the First Salmon ceremony. The sheer number of nets endangered navigation on the Columbia. Salmon were literally being filtered out of the ocean. Salmon runs began to dwindle. Seals were observed feasting on salmon at river mouths; riflemen were hired to purge these competitors, but this didn't appreciably increase the salmon runs. By the turn of the century, the smart operators were moving to new grounds in Alaska. For them, as for the whale captains and seal hunters who had gone before, the coast had lost its reason for existence.

By the 1930s, a fish far smaller and less glamorous than salmon had transformed Monterey into one of the world's largest fishing complexes. This new jackpot was the sardine. At its peak the catch amounted to 700,000 tons a year. Then both the catch and the size of the fish declined, even as fishing equipment became more advanced. The California Department of Fish and Game warned that the sardine industry was destroying its very livelihood through overfishing . . . but to no avail. The Department warned the State Legislature that a valuable marine resource was being depleted . . . to little avail. A moratorium on sardine fishing was finally enacted only when there were so few fish that no industry remained to protest the restraint on itself. Much of the Monterey canneries' equipment was sold to companies in South America. The cannery buildings themselves have been converted into luxury restaurants that serve lobster imported from Africa and Australia. And fishery officials are now seeking for clauses in current regulations to protect the declining California halibut and Pacific mackerel stocks. A moratorium on Pacific mackerel fishing has recently been adopted.

One marine bonanza didn't require the use of a single boat. An ordinary shovel would do to harvest pismo clams from the sand. This wasn't efficient enough, however, for one man who brought a plow and a team of horses down to the seashore to dig up clams that would go into feed for chickens and hogs. This enterprise turned the shore into what looked like the scene of a national plowing contest —and then there weren't enough pismo clams left to justify it. Today, plowing for pismo clams is prohibited.

In 1841 James Dana, a member of the U. S. Naval Exploratory Expedition, reported in a survey of the rugged coastal ranges, "The forests may be felled more easily than the mountains, and notwithstanding their size, they will not long bid defiance to the hearty ax men of America." By the time marine hunters had run through the otter, the seals, the gray whales, and the salmon, logging was in full swing. The coastal forests presented the greatest challenge ever posed to the lumbering industry. Cutting through the massive trunks was a task so big that for a time dynamite was used instead of saws. Once cut, the huge logs had to be transported to the sawmill. In the east, gentle slopes and deep-flowing rivers made this relatively easy. Snow on the ground helped as a log slide. But here the gradients were steep, snow falls were only local and the rivers were capricious, shrinking from a flood in spring to a trickle in late summer. And redwood had an unobliging tendency to sink rather than float.

Yet neither tree girth nor terrain could confound the sawteeth of the lumbering industry. Having largely denuded the east, the midwest and the south of their forests, the lumbermen found ways of slashing into those of the far west. If no natural transportation system existed, one could be improvised. Forests were cut not only for the market but to form "skid roads," over which logs could be hauled or pushed to the mill. Since horses and donkeys weren't strong enough to haul these logs, oxen were imported by the boxcar. The oxen sufficed . . . but only for a while. Steam engines were harnessed to haul logs; then came geared locomotives, and finally huge trucks. Bulldozers carved out road networks so that the trucks could form a conveyor line between forest and sawmill. A crescendo of mechanical sounds drowned out wind songs and bird calls, as logs by the thousand tumbled down from coastal slopes. At the sawmills there was now the problem of where to store all the logs. Gradually the waters of Puget Sound, Coos Bay, and Humboldt Bay disappeared beneath huge rafts of logs, and the shorefront disappeared beneath piles of lumber and mounds of sawdust. The wet wilderness that had once been a prison for Lewis and Clark was now no more than a lumber factory. What didn't serve the needs of lumbering had no right to exist. Beds of shellfish and marsh grass were pounded to death by log rafts shifting with the tides. Pulp mill wastes added to domestic sewage befouled estuarine waters. Salmon that survived nets, dams, and outfalls reached their ancestral spawning beds only to find the gravel buried under silt from the denuded forest slopes. With the soil cover removed, mountains began tumbling along with the trees that covered them. Sparks from lumbering operations, as well as from lightning, now set forests afire, and these fires were worse because log slash added further kindling. Summer might dispel the coastal clouds, but smoke from coastal conflagrations could still shut out the sun. Amid these conflagrations, fleeting encounters might occur between man and nature. An Oregon author, J. Larry Kemp, told how during one fire, two volunteer firefighters "were forced by the crowning flames to retreat into the Wilson River at Devil's Ford. The two young men were immediately followed by a herd of black-tailed deer and a cougar, all bent on self-preservation and paying no attention to anything else. When the fires passed over, deer, men, and cat each went his own way, completely ignoring the others."

Mudflats as well as forests became a bonanza as garbage collectors competed to transform tidelands into dumps. Many developers were glad to have the tidelands filled in to make way for housing tracts. Dredges ("mud mills") were imported from the Atlantic and Gulf seaboards to hasten the conversion of mudflats. From Puget Sound to San Diego Bay, shorelines shrank and wetlands disappeared. By 1966, with tideland developers rolling out man-made lands as easily as a layer of sod, California had been able to convert two-thirds of all its estuarine land. One day a scientist engaged in a national estuarine survey breezed into Oregon and asked marine biologist Joel Hedgpeth how he would classify the nearby Yaquina Bay. Hedgpeth said he knew of just one universal classification for estuaries: "shrinking."

To make up for the Pacific coast's unobliging lack of harbors, the builders of Los Angeles early converted its islands and channeled mudflats into a major industrial port. Communities up and down the coast joined the competition by promoting harbors and marinas of their own. A rash of breakwaters and jetties along the shore gave protection not only to tankers but also to even the most modest of sailboats. The slightest concavity along the shore would be promoted as a harbor, often one intended strictly for pleasure boats—thus opening up rich new opportunities for dredging and for federal contracts. Structures to improve the shore tended to hold up the natural transport of sand along the littoral. As jetties proliferated, downcoast beach owners saw their sandy front yards vanish; upcoast beach owners saw their beaches fan out like miniature deserts, and harbors filled up with sand. Instead of a harbor, boat owners could find themselves prisoners in a boat basin they had paid to occupy. At Santa Cruz, sandbars that keep the harbor closed for up to three months each year have become a picnic site. When dredges reopen the harbor, the picnic sites vanish but another hazard to navigation remains: the displaced sandbars now produce waves of the kind that brings surfers flocking to the shore.

In the effort to preserve the configuration of the shore, dredging for construction was superseded by dredging for maintenance. The ubiquitous dredge became as common as an ocean sunset. Long truck convoys periodically restore beaches, competing with construction firms for deposits of sand. By late 1973, Surfside-Sunset Beach in southern California had acquired its third artificial beach. Inland dams and an upcoast jetty block the natural supply of sand. The erosive effect of the jetty extends twelve miles downcoast and jeopardizes a four-lane highway, property developments valued at $100 million, and four public beaches including the most popular in all of California. The U. S. Army Corps of Engineers estimates that over the next hundred years, this sandy shore will require thirty million cubic yards of sand. Where that amount of sand will come from, nobody knows.

The restructuring of the shore with harbors and filled-in land paved the way for more urbanization. In California 90 percent of the population inhabit 8 percent of the land. This land lies adjacent to the shore and is occupied by such major cities as San

Francisco, Oakland, Los Angeles, and San Diego. Along the coast of southern California, the population averages 2600 persons per square mile, or twenty times the state's average density of 124 persons per square mile. As population and industry rise, so do wasteloads, making estuaries a hazard to public health, turning shellfish into living vials of poison, and raising the specter of increased sewage treatment costs. With that specter, once again, yet another bonanza has emerged—a convenient method of shortcutting waste treatment costs propounded in 1957 by A M Rawn, a sanitation official with Los Angeles County and chairman of the California State Water Pollution Control Board:

> If the ocean, or one of its arms, can be reached with a sewer outfall, within the bounds of economy, the specter of an extensive, complete treatment plant grows dimmer and dimmer and dimmer until it fades entirely and, to the great satisfaction of those who have to gather funds for the public budget (as well as you and I who have to pay the bill), the good old ocean does the job for free.

Thus, as aqueducts lengthened to divert water from remote wilderness watersheds to the arid coast, there was also a lengthening of outfalls into the Pacific, the new sewage concealment plant. One Los Angeles outfall was seven miles long. The Pacific Ocean was now "useful" for domestic and industrial purposes. Two decades later, however, the board that Rawn had once chaired was forced to upgrade discharge standards to ensure that such outfalls did not impair the biological productivity of the California Current. The outfall systems have come under investigation as possible "disease epicenters." A marked rise in finrot disease in one species of fish has been correlated with its degree of proximity to outfall discharges. This is ominous. Even more ominous is the limited degree of our knowledge of the marine environment, despite the presumptuous assertions that we can "conquer the ocean"—a knowledge so limited that marine scientists have difficulty in distinguishing between natural and pollution-induced diseases in fish—or a combination of the two. The ocean may indeed "do the job for free," but only if its life-giving processes are considered expendable.

Today, little more than a century since the arrival of the first dredges, axes, and outfalls, the Pacific shore is an industrialists' and engineers' dream come true, altered and rearranged to produce commerce, lumber, real estate and oil. At the same time, the Pacific shore has grown old and sick before its time. The coastal Indians, once scorned for their lack of enterprise, had passed on an environment with its natural productivity intact. Today this priceless legacy is in disarray. The potlatch has been turned upside down; our industrial triumphs celebrate stilled waves, depleted fisheries, and treeless slopes.

As the illusion of solidity, of endless productivity ebbs, the Faustian nature of the shore, the traps and pitfalls it contains for an exploitative mentality, become more evident. The millions of dollars expended to dredge out countless harbors are on the way to being exceeded by the millions of dollars required to protect our beaches from harbor jetties. California is the nation's leading recipient of federal disaster relief—much of which is no more than the financing of a return engagement as cities rebuild on the coastal flood plains, the fault zones and the unstable hillsides that court natural disaster.

The cost of upsetting the natural integrity of the Pacific shore, of forever restabilizing the coast, of losing shellfish beds to contamination, is climbing into the millions. The more the various departments of public works scurry about to "stabilize" this illusive environment, the less permanent it seems to become. So much frantic activity suggests a man in ill-fitting clothes who is constantly hitching up his pants, pulling on his hat, adjusting his tie and tucking in his shirt, as though that were all he needed.

Today, corporate advertisements already depict thriving cities, military bases, and mines in the next "frontier," the ocean bed. Submarines in all sizes and shapes shuttle among these technological visions, along with a lost fish or two. Yet the very corporations and government agencies that are now rushing to be in on the "Conquest of the Ocean" stumble over the jetties, the bulkheads, the "No Trespassing" and quarantine signs, on a shore that is already conquered. Before we conquer the ocean, that shore may bankrupt us.

We meticulously oil, overhaul, and tune up the machinery that alters the shore to our specifications —machinery that has been unleashed with little recognition for the delicate yet inexorable processes that maintain beaches, marine animals, and coastal forests. Perhaps the coastal and submarine forests have been too silent. If they purred like an engine and sputtered when something jammed or went out of order, perhaps we would have recognized their true nature sooner. Perhaps.

Whitman's "grander future" has turned out to be a miscalculation. The peoples along the Pacific shore have reached a high standard of living—and cheapened the environment in which they enjoy it. The men and women who explored the Pacific shore, who learned to exploit its wealth, and who continue to reshape it, have exhibited some admirable qualities: courage, dedication, ingenuity. But those qualities are contravened by the narrowness of their goals. John Steinbeck, the author, and Ed Ricketts, a marine naturalist, who lived in the Monterey area when the sardine bonanza was in full swing, foresaw its outcome. On a marine collecting expedition to the Gulf of California, they were shocked to find a similar boom under way: the Japanese were fishing intensively for shrimp, with the approval of Mexican officials. Steinbeck and Ricketts wrote:

Perhaps we might find a parallel in a moving picture company such as Metro-Goldwyn-Mayer. The units are superb—great craftsmen, fine directors, the best actors in the profession—and yet due to some overlying expediency, some impure or decaying quality, the product of these good units is sometimes vicious, sometimes stupid, sometimes inept, and never as good as the men who make it. The Mexican official and the Japanese captain were both good men, but by their association in the project directed honestly or dishonestly by forces behind and above them, they were committing a true crime against nature and against the immediate welfare of Mexico and the eventual welfare of the human species.

The excesses of exploitation have led to a growing body of laws that regulate lumbering, fishing, tideland reclamation, sewage disposal, and the recovery of oil. Indeed, the states along the Pacific shore may very well have the most extensive set of such regulations in the world. These regulations, although they mitigate the excesses of exploitation, fail to resolve basic problems. The demand for resources often exceeds our capacity to effectively regulate or control it. Writing of the many humanly caused forces working to disrupt the natural transport of sand, Dr. Douglas Inman of Scripps Institution of Oceanography remarks, "We are in the curious position of developing and improving beach frontage without criteria for predicting changes in the beach or evaluating the likelihood of the beaches' existence in ten or twenty years."

Scientists themselves can be overwhelmed by the task of understanding our effect on the Pacific shore. In a study by marine scientists on the impact of massive withdrawals of ocean water to cool a coastal nuclear power plant, one focused on the mortality of plankton entrained in the cooling system. The study showed the mortality to be relatively low. However, some scientists at Scripps Institution of Oceanography who reviewed these optimistic results, including Dr. James Enright and Dr. John McGowan, found that test procedures utilized in the study indicated only that some cells in a planktonic organism were alive, not the entire organism. By these procedures, raw meat at the supermarket would be classified as alive. One scientist commented, "I've never heard of a live salami." These dubious results were submitted to a California regulatory board composed of laymen who had no way of evaluating them. The study had been financed and organized by a major proponent of the nuclear plant, Southern California Edison Company. The results suggest that protecting the environment is too important to be left to those who are bent on altering it.

The many complications of our impact on the Pacific shore can shake even the best of scientists. One well-known expert has expressed serious concern about the scientific validity of some standards applied to ocean discharges, suggesting that these standards may lead to the costly overdesign of outfall systems, and has helped spearhead a study that recommended less strict standards. Some of his academic colleagues pointed out, however, that his study methods were not above scientific question either. Asked whether he wished to be listed as the primary author of the study report, he replied, "You can blame me for the report, but please don't credit me with it."

Amid such perplexing developments, the psychology of the Big Bonanza continues to flourish, as new fixations replace the old. The same relentless drive that led to whale-killing binges, salmon net wars, and pismo clam plowing, has closed in more recently on offshore oil reservoirs. The mere emplacement of legs for one offshore oil platform opened up natural oil seeps, clearly indicating a weak and fractured geological stratum. Despite this warning, platform drilling was begun. Months later, oil gushed up through this weak stratum and resulted in the blowout in the Santa Barbara Channel. Citizens with tarred boats, bathers who could no longer enjoy the shore, and fishermen whose nets were fouled with oil, had become the latterday kin of the coastal Indians whose salmon rivers and rain forests were exploited and sacrificed by our forefathers.

Today, the prospect of a bonanza is often packaged as a "crisis" to encourage regulatory leniency. Thus, the energy crisis has brought renewed pressures for drilling in the Santa Barbara Channel.

Yet to the risks of a geological fault are now added those caused by man. Two shipping lanes in the channel, which cut through a total of thirty-four federal offshore leases, carry oil tankers en route to Los Angeles. These foggy waters, studded with rocky islets, have already claimed a hundred shipwrecks. Yet mobile drilling rigs are still permitted to operate up to the boundaries of the shipping lanes, in an intimacy that is hardly reassuring when the current tankers' record of navigation is considered, along with the prospect that Alaskan oil tankers may soon be added to the traffic through these same shipping lanes.

The channel, with its bustle of drilling rigs, happens to lie between the Navy Missile range at Point Mugu and the Vandenberg Missile Range, operated by the Air Force. It is here that the Navy has tried out heat-seeking rockets. An oil executive told the *Los Angeles Times,* "One of the things that bothers us is that those things were designed to sink the very sort of vessel we're drilling from"— a rather unpatriotic aspersion on military marksmanship. A Navy pilot fresh from Vietnam managed to cut loose a Bullpup missile, which sank a Navy patrol vessel. Off-target missiles have twice ignited island brushfires. The U. S. government is not taking any chances. Federal leases in the channel stipulate that oil companies may not hold the United States responsible for any damage from errant or aborted missiles. There are even stipulations that oil operations are to be suspended and evacuated when the crossfire becomes particularly intense. Oil personnel can be evacuated, but it may be tough to evacuate oil platforms. One sometimes wonders whether the oil industry and the Pentagon are responsible to anyone more predicatble than W. C. Fields!

As public officials try to upgrade the quality of marine water along the Pacific coast, the presence of oil becomes more pervasive, sparing no mortals. In 1971, a Navy tanker spilled oil off southern California, coating the presidential sands at San Clemente. Some oil got on the coat of King Timahoe, the Commander-in-Chief's Irish setter. But in many respects the spill was routine. The Navy first denied it, then admitted to a refueling operation that had spilled 1200 gallons, and finally revised the figure to 229,446 gallons. Efforts to control the pollution centered, at least in press releases, around a much-vaunted oil skimmer, "a kind of sea sweeper," which was completed by the time Marines had finished laundering the presidential sands by hand. Amid this display of prowess in antipollution, President Nixon had to avoid the beach —an adjustment that echoes the advice a Greek shipping magnate is reported to have offered British officials concerned with spill-control: "Let them build swimming pools."

Chapter 5

Pacific Shore Modern

Newspaper articles in 1973 dealt with a pioneering surfer and with a pioneering user of electronic metal detectors on the beaches of southern California—who happened to be the same person, one Delbert "Bud" Higgins. The progression in his career from surfer to metal detecting beachcomber suggests a progression in response to a changing habitat.

Agile surfers had been riding the waves of Hawaii, over a thousand miles from California, for centuries before the sport was taken up on its shores. In the 1920s, Hollywood movie companies imported the Hawaiian surfer Duke Kahanamoku to appear in their films. The Duke found good surfing at Corona Del Mar beach. The California natives, confronted by the exciting new prospect of riding a surfboard atop the waves, no longer found mere body surfing quite so exciting.

At the bathhouse where the Duke stored his board, a massive one by today's standards, Higgins and other would-be emulators studied it diligently. By the time the Duke had returned to Hawaii, boards were being shaped, sawed, planed, and sandpapered in dozens of California garages, backyards, and parking lots.

The original boards were made of redwood; they were heavy—about 135 pounds—two stories tall, and about three inches thick. They looked almost heavy enough to crush the waves they were made to ride on. An inner tube was used to keep one of them from bouncing and staving in the roof of the car that transported it. Getting the massive plank from the parking space to the surf line was one more strenuous task for a would-be surfer. Hunched under the massive board balanced on his back, he advanced with about the speed of a turtle towards the surf.

Like the earlier lumbermen, surfers learned how redwood can become waterlogged, so that a board weighing 135 pounds dry became twenty pounds heavier when it was wet. If the waves hadn't exhausted him, the surfer might find that returning to the car with his board very well could. However, the sensation of riding atop the waves made up for the burden afterward. The boards proliferated, and more surfing spots were discovered: Huntington Beach, Dana Cove, La Jolla, Rincon, Salt Creek, Malibu. But many of the young pioneer surfers, including Higgins, still favored Corona Del Mar. A long, smooth ride from the open ocean would carry one all the way into a bay cove. It could take thirty minutes to paddle back out to await the next wave. But what did that matter?

Today Higgins stalks the beaches with his metal detector, uncovering rings, pennies, watches, and other objects inadvertently dropped by summer crowds. To avoid them, Higgins does his stalking at night or in predawn hours. It is a hobby, not a profession. Even though one couple unearthed $600 in a single year, the interest of the Internal

Revenue Service has not been piqued . . . yet. Beach metal detecting is wonderful exercise, particularly if you are in your sixties and still like to be outdoors. You walk along the sand, seeing the gulls and the waves, bending perhaps fifty or sixty times to unearth pennies, dimes, medallions, or nails. One of Higgins' friends has done enough bending to collect one hundred rings, including some set with diamonds and jade. In the wake of a coastal storm, the magnetic scavengers will hustle down to the eroded beaches in the hope of discovering Liberty-head dimes, dropped perhaps decades before.

Sometimes, in the predawn hours, Higgins watches young men surfing by pierlight—a fond reminder of forty years ago. And yet, even if Higgins could have his youth back and march into the surf again, he would find that something has gone out of the sport in which he was a pioneer. The waves are still just as accommodating. The boards, made of synthetic materials, are not only lighter but shorter and thinner, as well as waterproof and vastly more maneuverable. Today's surfer carries his board under his arm and transports it atop his car like a pair of skis. The waters are no colder; in fact, today's surfer can wear a wet suit and surf the year round.

The sport of surfing has improved immeasurably —except for one essential. If Higgins were to go down to Corona Del Mar today, he would see the long, rolling waves of his youth reduced to mere large ripples by a harbor development. If he went to Dana Cove, he would find a huge boat garage encircled by a rock breakwater that blocks the free run of the waves. Incredibly, surfing waves can be as hard to find as sardines. Stimulated by surfing movies, surfing magazines, and by displays of surfing apparatus, young men seeking the same waves that Higgins enjoyed forty years ago now line up for the waves where jetties and No Trespassing signs have not yet intruded. In their quest for waves, they descend on public beaches where they encounter zoning regulations that protect the thousands of body surfers and waders who compete for a place in the same water. For those who can afford it, there are global tours. Surfing can become an endless search of unpredictable outcome for access to free-running waves.

People who go to the shore in search of natural values are in trouble today, and surfers, even with their lightweight boards, their wet suits, and their sports cars, meet with obstacles that Higgins, with his redwood board, didn't have to worry about. People who depend on man-made pleasures are in a much better position, and thus Higgins with his metal detector is very much the modern beach man, adapted to the changing shore. His electronic recreation cannot be jeopardized by jetties, breakwaters, and other manipulations of the shore. Indeed, the consequences of shore improvement can enhance his chosen pastime. Beaches that must depend on continually hauling in sand to withstand the erosion produced by upcoast jetties offer a rapid turnover to the owners of metal detectors.

The sheer crush of numbers enhances the value of such a hobby. As more people swarm to the beaches, the quantity of coins and jewelry they drop there increases accordingly. In their affluence, people have more things to lose. Indeed, to be able to enjoy the beach, they must bring fistfuls of change for parking meters, concessions, and rentals. The beach is one of the last holdouts against the credit card. While the body surfers and the board surfers compete in this crush of numbers, Higgins, with his flashlight, can wait for dawn, night, or winter. His pastime is largely immune to polluted water, crowded parking lots, beach erosion, and, thanks to his metal-detecting earphones, even noise pollution. (The lifeguards' headquarters at one Los Angeles beach must be soundproofed because of commercial jets overhead.)

My nine-year-old son is losing interest in sand castles. He is learning to ride a raft in the surf. Occasionally he'll watch me body surf, or, when I go skin diving, he'll rush down as I come ashore to ask what I saw. I'm anxious to show him how to skin dive and body surf as he grows older. But he also watches the board surfers. He notices the kind of swim trunks that are "in," the waxed and painted designs on the surf boards, and he listens as they tell each other about waves caught or missed. When he is out rafting on the waves, he's thinking of board surfing, not body surfing.

He will want to seek out the same waves that Higgins pursued forty years ago. By the time he is ten, he will be ready with his own surfboard, the "in" kind of trunks, the tousled hair, the wet suit. I'll be the bystander then. In fact, until he's old enough to drive himself, I'll probably be prowling the coast with him in a car to seek out free-running waves. I could attempt to deter him from taking up this unpredictable sport, but I doubt that I could succeed. The magnetism of board surfing is such that young men will put up with a lot to get a shot at it. And yet somewhere down the road will there be too many marina jetties, too many No Trespassing signs, too many closed parking lots, too many electric gates, too many surfing restrictions?

Surfing looks more promising in Arizona, where an entrepreneur has set up a wave machine in a basin suitable for somewhat truncated surf rides. The wave action is man-made in a controlled environment, safe from the whims of jetty builders and developers. A resourceful entrepreneur can offer a beach complete with dunes. The sands might even be sown with metal slugs, to be redeemed as prizes at a metal-detection concession. No beach erosion, no quarantine signs. You could call it Desert Surfers' Paradise, or even Pacific Shore II.

The seemingly inexorable forces that bear down on free-flowing waves and open beaches can also doom other coastal features. Along the central California coast, a strip only three to five miles wide is blessed with a unique combination of rich soil, rain cycles, and marine air that keeps the climate moderate. Here 60 percent of the brussels sprouts, 70 percent of the broccoli and 95 percent of the artichokes consumed in America are produced. All of this could vanish within ten or fifteen years.

As of 1973, one acre of land planted to brussels sprouts could bring in approximately $1047. However, land along the central California coast was being valued at $2500 an acre and taxed at this rate. Housing developers found that they could make more money by using these rich soils as tract

pads. As a result, 75 percent of the acreage planted to brussels sprouts in one coastal county was being leased by previous owners from corporate speculators who could afford to pay the taxes while awaiting the opportune time for residential subdivision. How could lands so valuable for food production be displaced for a use that had no need for a rich soil? In coastal California, one of two houses, similar in style and within two or three blocks of each other, may sell for $60,000, the other for $150,000. There is a difference of $90,000 in the price because one fronts on the coast and the other doesn't. The same market forces that doom brussels sprouts can result in closing off a beachfront for luxury residential use. In a report for the State of California, the planning firms of Sedway/Cooke and Gruen & Associates made the forecast "that undoubtedly the coastal zone will eventually become one huge linear residential development with gaps in it that the present system of land use allocation is not modifying in some way."

Can technology produce fields of brussels sprouts and artichokes inland as well as it has simulated surfing waves in Arizona? A coastal climate might be duplicated through irrigation, greenhouses, and air conditioning . . . at the cost of $100,000 an acre. That is why brussels sprouts, broccoli, and artichokes may one day become as scarce as sardines now are along the Pacific shore.

Through increasing the value of adjacent land *forty times over,* coastal freeway routings have automatically brought the kiss of death to coastal agriculture and other low-density uses along the coast. Whatever public beaches remain are usurped by public parking lots as surf is wedded to asphalt.

The relentless obliteration of such coastal values, although often regretted, has been accepted as an inevitable casualty of progress. The search for a bonanza has become so incessant in our way of life that it appears to have acquired a separate existence, with a momentum of its own, that is beyond our power to reform or control. The same people who take televised space walks for granted find themselves enmeshed in the modern equivalent of a Greek tragedy, its two-car standard of consumption hurtling as though preordained towards sandless beaches, oil-polluted bays, shrinking estuaries, and movies about surfers.

In such a predicament, one can hear the laughter of the Yurok Indians that Carl Meyer caught himself feeling sorry for. Without a single oil well or power boat, these former residents managed to enjoy leisure within the same coastal environment that had sustained their culture for over three thousand years. Others from the more recent past have recognized the wisdom of that native culture; their voices, likewise, are now becoming audible—if not yet heeded.

Chapter 6

The Shore in Literature

While he explored the Pacific shore for the rulers of England in 1792, Captain George Vancouver made the unpolitical observation that "to describe the beauties of this region will, on some future occasion, be a very grateful task of a skillful panegyrist."

The challenge of that "very grateful task" has drawn a response from some of the world's finest writers. What is perhaps most striking about their work is that it reflected—in ways that were often prophetic—the growing conflict between exploitation and natural values. Indeed, the artistic eye is forced to look ever more closely, not at the nature of the shore, but at the nature of the people living beside it.

The early explorers, although they sensed the natural magnificence of the shore, were after all prepared to view wilderness not as the source of an esthetic experience but as a thing to be conquered and developed for the sake of God, king, and/or their own advantage. There was little to be gained by admiring the stateliness of the coastal redwood, the roll of Pacific combers, or the vertical thrust of wave-battered cliffs. Yet these hard-pressed adventurers, with their digestive systems and their nerves often in an uproar, did acknowledge the imposing character of the coastal scene. It was with a mixture of exaltation and fear that Juan Rodriguez Cabrillo, passing the Santa Lucia range, wrote of "mountains which reach the sky" and of

how "it seemed as if [they] would fall upon the ships."

The Lewis and Clark expedition reached the mouth of the Columbia River only to be confronted by endless rains and log-encumbered waves. "The immense waves now break over the place where we were encamped, and the large trees, some of them five or six feet thick, which had lodged at the point, were drifted over our camp, and the utmost vigilance of every man could scarcely save our canoes from being crushed to pieces. . . . Yet, though wet and cold, and some of them sick from using the salt-water, the men are cheerful, and full of anxiety to see more of the ocean."

To a visitor in 1835, the Pacific coast could produce exhilaration as well as awe. In a respite from loading hides aboard a trading vessel, Richard Henry Dana found himself at what is now Dana Point—a scene that inspired in him a mood far different from that aroused by the grease-covered seal hunters he had observed in San Francisco Bay:

There was a grandeur in everything around which gave a solemnity to the scene, a silence and solitariness which affected every part. Not a human being but ourselves for miles, and no sound heard but the pulsations of the great Pacific. And the great steep hill rising like a wall and cutting us from all the world but the "world of waters." I separated myself from the rest and sat down on a rock, just where the sea ran in and formed a fine spouting horn. Compared with the dull sand beach of the coast, this grandeur was as refreshing as a great rock in a weary land. It was almost the first time that I had been positively home since I left home. My better nature returned strong upon me. Everything was in accordance with my state of feeling, and I experienced a glow of pleasure at finding that what of poetry and romance I have ever had in me had not been entirely deadened.

Twenty-four years later, the author of *Two Years Before the Mast* revisited California. It was a bittersweet reunion; Dana regretted having left the sea for the life of a lawyer on shore. "The truth is I was made for the sea," Dana wrote to his wife. "It suits me, and I am always content when on it. I believe I was intended for a sailor. My life on shore is a mistake." The southern California shore inspired him once again . . . except for one jarring note.

Little is it altered—the same repose and the golden sunlight and glorious climate, sheltered by its hills: and then, more remindful than anything else, the roars and tumbles upon the beach, the same grand surf of the great Pacific as on the beautiful day when the *Pilgrim,* after her five-months voyage, dropped her weary anchors here; the same bright blue ocean, and the surf making just the same monotonous and melancholy roar, and the same dreamy town and gleaming white mission, as when we beached our boats for the first time, riding over the breakers with shouting Kanakas, the three small hidetraders lying at anchor in the offing. But now we are the only vessel, and that an unromantic, sail-less, spar-less, engine-driven hulk!

At Pueblo de Los Angeles, Dana again acknowledged the spell of the coast:

The wife of Don Juan, who was a beautiful young girl when we were on the coast, Doña Refugio, daughter of Don Santiago Arguello, the Commandant of San Diego, was with him, and still handsome. This is one of several instances I have noticed of the preserving quality of the California climate.

In 1873 David Berry, a visitor to Santa Barbara, observed: "Near Santa Barbara vast quantities of petroleum rise to the surface of the sea and overspread and perfume a large area. Our recollections of good Santa Barbara will be that she was a messenger of peace pouring oil upon the troubled waters."

In the midst of a transcontinental love affair, Robert Louis Stevenson stopped over in Monterey, where the beauty of the shore was sufficient to make him forget his preoccupation.

The one common note of all this country is the haunting presence of the ocean. A great faint sound of breakers follows you high up into the inland canyons; the roar of waters dwells in the clean, empty rooms of Monterey as in a shell upon the chimney. The woods and the Pacific rule between them the climate of the seaboard region. On the streets of Monterey, when the air does not smell salt from the one it will be blowing perfumed from the resinous tree tops of the other.

The coastal fogs that had played havoc with navigators did likewise with Stevenson's tubercular condition. As a writer, nevertheless, he found them inspiring:

At sunset, for months together, vast wet, melancholy fogs arise and come shoreward from the ocean. From the hilltop above Monterey the scene is often noble, although it is always sad. The upper air is still bright with sunlight; a glow still rests upon the Gabelano Peak; but the fogs are in possession of the lower level; they crawl in scarves among the sandhills; they float, a little higher, in clouds of a gigantic size and often of a wild configuration; to the south, where they have struck the seaward shoulder of the mountains of Santa Lucia, they double back and spire skyward like smoke. Where their shadow touches, color dies out of the world. The air grows chill and deadly as they advance. The trade-wind freshens, the trees begin to sigh, and all the windmills in Monterey are whirling and creaking and filling their cisterns with the brackish water of the sands. It takes but a little while till the invasion is complete. The sea, in its lighter order, has submerged the earth.

Long before the planners and marine engineers, Stevenson had sensed that the shore is a meeting place, rather than a dividing line, for natural forces of sea and land.

Farther north, another British visitor wrote of

discovering the charm of the Oregon shore: "I have lived! The American continent may now sink under the sea for I have taken the best that it yields, and the best was neither dollars, love, nor real estate." That best was—catching a salmon. As the fisherman, Rudyard Kipling, described the experience:

I went into that icy cold river and made my cast just above a weir, and all but foul-hooked a blue and black water snake with a coral mouth who coiled herself on a stone and hissed maledictions. The next cast—ah, the pride of it, the regal splendor of it! The thrill that ran down from finger-tip to toe! The water boiled. He broke for the spoon and got it! . . . There be several sorts of success in this world that taste well in the moments of enjoyment, but I question whether the stealthy theft of a line from an able-bodied salmon who knows exactly what you are doing and why you are doing it is not sweeter than any other victory within human scope.

Back at Monterey, a more lethargic form of life launched a native-born poet into whimsy. This was George Sterling, in "The Abalone Song":

O! Some folks boast of quail on toast,
Because they think it's toney;
But I'm content to owe rent,
And live on abalone.

Some stick to biz, some flirt
Down on the sands at Coney;
But we, by hell! stay in Carmel,
And nail the abalone.

He hides in caves beneath the waves—
His ancient patrimony,
And so, 'tis shown that faith alone
Reveals the abalone.

The more we take, the more they make
In deep-sea matrimony;
Race-suicide cannot betide
The fertile abalone.

The Pacific shore, despite its relatively late discovery, rapidly became world-famous through the prose of Dana, Stevenson, and Kipling and through the work of talented photographers. What they proclaimed was that the Pacific shore offered more than quick profits—that it could refresh, enliven, and inspire the human spirit, yielding qualities that no favorable roll of the economic dice could ever provide . . . and do so free of charge. In 1859 J. Ross Browne, a frontier treasury agent, found himself temporarily stranded in a northern California coastal community. From a sparse collection of wooden buildings to which someone had given the pretentious name of Crescent City, Browne turned his gaze to the sea:

The sea is so vast and broad here, the surf rolls in with such a grand rebound over the craggy shore; the white seagulls soar aloft over the cliffs with such a graceful freedom; and all nature has such a comprehensive aspect—stretching so far away from the petty vexations of life, that there is nothing left in me of envy, jealousy, malice or hatred; nothing but love for the good, true, and pure.

Continually interspersed with such visions were other visions of vast wealth—salmon, lumber, gold, or oil. That these two themes might conflict was recognized early. In 1889 John Muir, a visitor more accustomed to the magnetism of Sierra peaks, wrote in fascination of Puget Sound:

Water and sky, mountain and forest, clad in sunshine and clouds, are composed in landscapes sublime in magnitude, yet exquisitely fine and fresh, and full of glad, rejoicing life. The shining waters stretch away into the leafy wilderness, now like the reaches of some majestic river and again expanding into broad roomy spaces like mountain lakes, their farther edges fading gradually and blending with the pale blue of the sky.

At the same time, Muir sensed at work a force no less awesome than wilderness itself:

She [Puget Sound] also is already rich in busy workers, who work hard, though not always wisely, hacking, burning, blasting their way deeper into the wilderness, beneath the sky, and beneath the ground. The wedges of development are being driven hard, and none of the obstacles or defenses of nature can long withstand the onset of this immeasurable industry.

Stevenson had felt similar misgivings: "California has been a land of promise in its time, like

64

(continued on page 81)

AT THE TIDE

There are good things to see in the tidepools and there are exciting and inter-esting thoughts to be generated from the seeing. Every new eye applied to the peephole which looks out at the world may fish in some new beauty and some new pattern and the world of the human mind must be enriched by such fishing.
—Edward F. Ricketts *Between Pacific Tides*

Only the protected estuaries and closed bays (San Diego or San Francisco are examples) are relatively uninfluenced by the relentless force of the sea. Sheltered coasts, rich in marine animals and concave in shape, such as Monterey Bay or Laguna, California, are protected by headlands, sandbars or islands.

(above) Giant blue-green anemone. Of all the creatures of the low intertidal rocks, the most conspicuous and exquisite is the giant blue-green anemone.

Kelp. After a summer's growing season, the first strong swells of autumn tear loose large bundles of offshore kelp. These are threshed by the surf, and finally, after being winnowed by the wind, the bits and pieces are deposited upon the shore in decaying piles, some to become rime-covered *(left)*.

Offshore, the great beds of kelp shelter countless creatures: baitfish like anchovies; bass, barracuda, yellowtail, and salmon; seals, and such passive dwellers as jellyfish, nudibranchs, bryozoans, limpets, urchins, and many species of epiphytic algae.

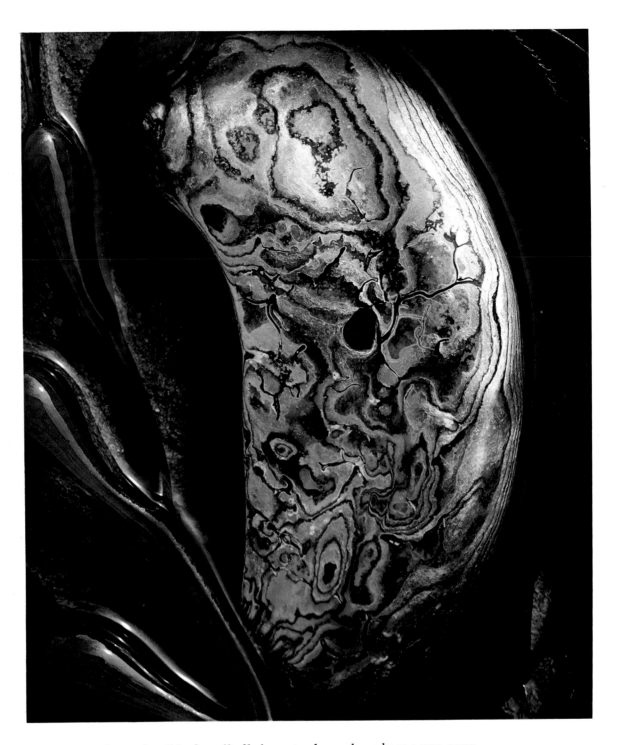

Surf-worn and gravel-polished until all the outer layers have been worn away, this shell once belonged to the great red abalone. The Pacific shore boasts eight species of abalone, although the great red is the preferred table species and is found from Cape Arago in southern Oregon south to San Diego.

(left) Shell litter, Pt. Piños, Monterey, California. In winter, exposed north- and northwest-facing beaches are good places to beachcomb after a storm. Prevailing southerly currents carry the sea's offerings downshore; high tides and a vigorous winter storm usually cast up something of interest.

(overleaf, left) Eroded rock, limpets and turban snails. In the deepest troughs where water remains the longest, colonies of anemones have established themselves and are joined by black and brown turban snails, and grazing limpets.

(overleaf, right) Chitons, La Jolla, California.

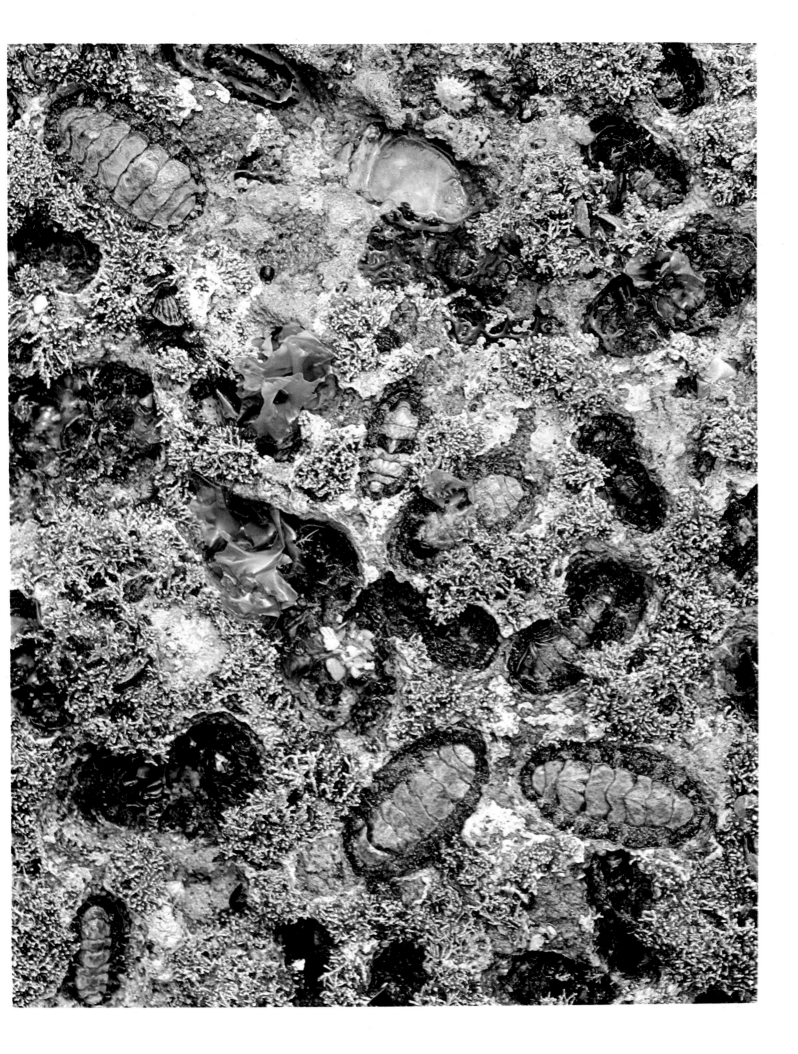

Barnacles and limpets, Pt. Loma, California. The young rock barnacles encrust the shells of a mature volcano barnacle and an owl limpet. Although the volcano barnacle feeds by thrusting up feathery food-gathering antennae when covered by high-tide waters, the owl limpet actively grazes, leaving its particular rock scar to browse. Each limpet manages to return to its own rock scar when the tide goes out.

(left) Limpets on sandstone, middle tidal zone. Young ribbed limpets browse about over fossil-bearing sedimentary sandstone. In many parts of the Pacific, today's beaches lie upon remains of earlier beaches. It is not uncommon to find a living limpet adhering to the standstone-bearing fossil of its ancestors.

Splash-zone tidepool: algae and periwinkles. Each upper, or splash-zone, tidepool
has its own uniqueness. Periwinkles or other small snails are often conspicuous.
Pools that are shaded support tiny sponges; other, more open pools—like this
one—seem occupied only by green plants until close inspection reveals other life.

(*right*) Marsh grasses, Siletz Bay, Oregon. The bay, the mud flat, the estuary
contain the richest, most productive living community of organisms on earth.
Its relentless, purposeful destruction is one of the major tragedies of man in
the New World.

74

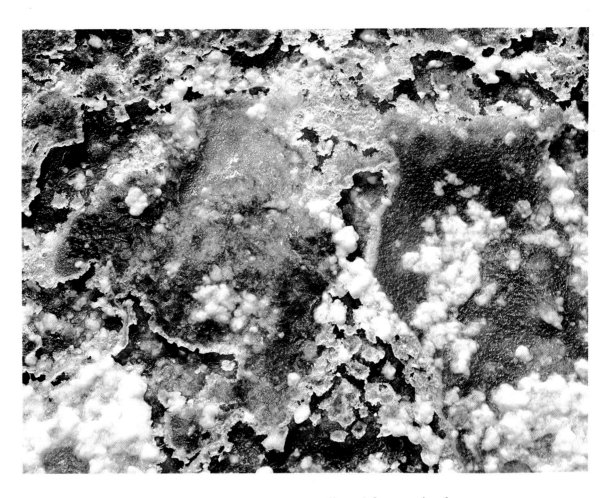

Salt crystals. Above the line of blue-green algae—the line of demarcation between what belongs to the sea and what does not—there are sometimes scattered pockets in the rock that collect the runoff of infrequent high surf, which evaporates, leaving inorganic salt.

(left) Driftwood at La Push, Olympic Peninsula, Washington.

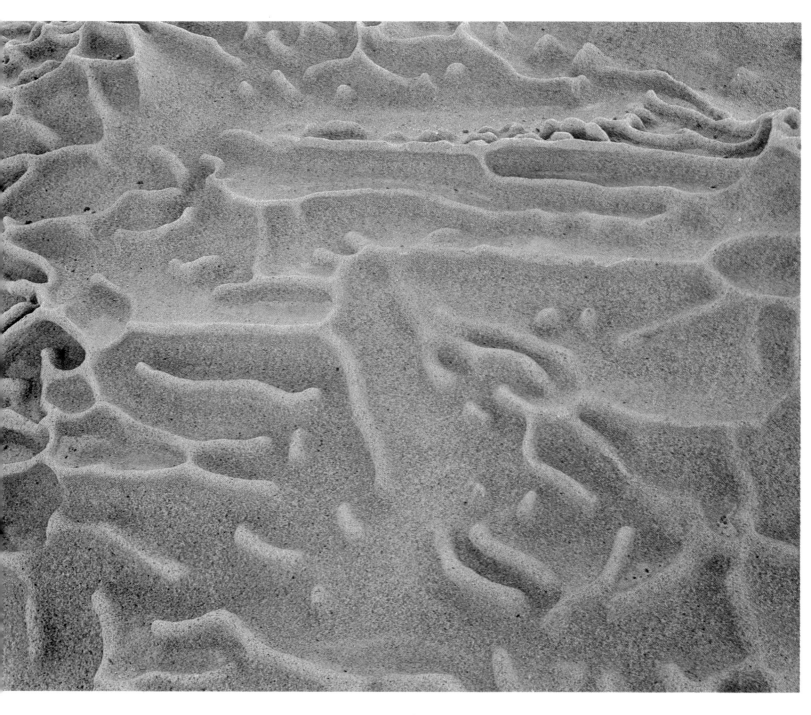

The sculptured beauty of wind and sea erosion, central California shore.

(right) Rockweeds of the upper tidal zones serve as the chief habitat of the periwinkles—creatures that cannot remain underwater without drowning.

Anemones, red encrusting sponge, and coralline algae on a sea cave floor. Here anemones rarely close their tentacles at low tide, as do exposed anemones. Hermit crabs, red and purple encrusting sponges, delicate hydroids and bryozoans are common.

(continued from page 64)

Palestine; but if the woods continue so swiftly to perish, it may become, like Palestine, a land of desolation." He wondered whether the state's two most famous natives, "redwood and redskins" could survive the ambitions of the "millionaire vulgarians of the Big Bonanza."

Horace Greeley was dismayed by the aftermath of hydraulic gold mining:

Earth distorted into all manner of ungainly heaps and ridges, hills half torn or washed away, and the residue left in as repulsive shape as can well be conceived, roads intersected and often turned to mire by ditches, water courses torn up and gouged out, and rivers, once pure as crystal, now dense and opaque with pulverized rock—such is the spectacle presented throughout the mining region. Not a stream of any size is allowed to escape the pollution —even the bountiful and naturally pure Sacramento is yellow with it, it flows turbid and uninviting to the Pacific.

Greeley visited California in 1859. Yet the sheer ferocity of industry was already evident:

Timber is wanted for flumes, for sluices, for drifts or tunnels, for dwellings, for running steam engines, etc., and as most of the land has no owner, everybody cuts and slashes as if he cared for nobody but himself, and no time but today. Patriarchal oaks are cut down merely to convert their limbs into fuel, leaving the trunks to rot. Noble pines are pitched this way and that, merely to take a log or two from the butt for sawing or splitting, leaving the residue a cumberer of the ground; trees fit for the noblest uses are made to subserve the paltriest, merely because they are handy and it is nobody's business to preserve them.

Jack London, who as a teen-ager had been fish warden in San Francisco Bay, later recalled the thrill of chasing a commercial fish pirate: "The huge sail, the howling wind, the driving seas, the plunging boat—I, a pygmy, a mere speck in the midst of it was mastering the elemental strife, flying through it and over it, triumphant and victorious." London then collided with a man-made contribution to the elemental strife: "And just then, as I roared along like a conquering hero, the boat received a frightful smash and came instantly to a dead stop. I was flung forward and into the bottom. As I sprang up I caught a fleeting glimpse of a greenish, barnacle-covered object, and knew it at once for what it was, that terror of navigation, a sunken pile."

As a frontier treasury agent investigating the misuse of federal funds, J. Ross Browne foresaw the relentless development that would bear down on the Pacific shore. As coastal communities "deprived" of natural harbors petitioned Congress for breakwaters to redress nature's oversight, Browne, in *Harper's New Monthly Magazine* for 1857, satirized such ambitions:

Taking into view the remarkable progress of California, it certainly is not anticipating too much to look forward to the day when Bear Harbor will be a great emporium of commerce and industry. At present it is true there is no way of reaching this favored locality except over Captain Toby's trails, which as I have already stated must have originally been intended for wild goats. Yet I do not regard that as an insufferable obstacle. Wherever goats can travel, so can public funds. The only difference is that the latter are a good deal harder to catch after they once get loose from the treasury. All that is needed is an appropriation from Congress.

Access to Bear Harbor by means of water would be easy enough if there was any harbor there. Vessels might then anchor when they arrived. Unfortunately, it is an open roadstead filled with rocks and presenting altogether a most frightful aspect in bad weather . . . Still, this cannot be regarded as any serious objection to federal enterprise. Have we not breakwaters in many places on our Atlantic coast where nature never intended commerce to exist and where, accordingly, none does and can ever exist?

Men like Stevenson, Muir and Greeley displayed a concern and an appreciation for the land that had seemingly vanished with the coastal Indians. Yet these men were not natives of the Pacific shore. Their existence did not depend on its natural bounty. They were conditioned by backgrounds many miles removed from the region: the soot-filled skies of Edinburgh and London, the devastated forests of the east, the squalid New York waterfront. Now they saw industry displaying a prowess never before seen on the globe, moving in on a natural beauty and grandeur that had only recently become known to the world. It was dismaying to realize that man could be no less wildly uncontrollable than the wilderness itself. The Pacific shore, because its development came so late, sharply dramatized issues that civilized man had not always acknowledged.

The seeming inability of men to control their own actions introduced a fatalism into the literature of the Pacific shore. Jack London, the fish warden turned novelist, railed against his countrymen as "they gobbled and gambled from the Atlantic to the Pacific, until they'd swined a whole continent. When they'd finished with the lands and forests and mines, they turned back, gambling for any little stakes they'd overlooked, gambling for franchises and monopolies . . ." Henry Miller, coming to the Carmel and Big Sur region a half century after Stevenson's visit, reported on the advance of the Big Bonanza psychology:

> Today Big Sur is no longer an outpost. The number of sightseers and visitors increases yearly. Emil White's *Big Sur Guide* alone brings swarms of tourists to our front door. What was inaugurated with virginal modesty threatens to end as a bonanza. The early settlers are dying off. Should their huge tracts of land be broken up into small holdings, Big Sur may rapidly develop into a suburb of Monterey, with bus service, barbecue stands, gas stations, chain stores and all the odious claptrap that makes suburbia horrendous.

Miller wondered whether the natural beauty that remained was under some sort of death sentence: "Often, when the clouds pile up in the north and the sea is churned with whitecaps, I say to myself: 'This is the California that men dreamed of years ago, this is the Pacific that Balboa looked out on from the peak of Darien, this is the face of the earth as the Creator intended it to look.'"

In bucolic Carmel, Sinclair Lewis, who as an aspiring novelist had once caroused with George Sterling and sold plots for stories to Jack London, returned after a fifteen-year interlude to "where once we went picknicking on the rocks, carrying our grub in baskets," but where "now they go over to the Del Monte Grill to dine and dance . . . and

those same once wild rocky shores, so free and uninhibited then, are covered with expensive houses. All in fifteen years!"

Abuse begins to inspire individual rebellions. A young San Diego reporter watched the grunion come ashore during high tide to spawn, only to be scooped up by the bucketful by earnest beach parties. When more were caught than could be eaten, the surplus was thrown away. In 1932 Max Miller wrote of them, in *I Cover the Waterfront:* "Being the waterfront reporter my job includes writing the story predicting the next grunion runs. But lately I have been growing mighty careless about this assignment. Mighty, mighty careless. The fish-and-game warden knows of my carelessness, but so far he has not told."

Such revulsion reached its climax in the poems of Robinson Jeffers, who had come to Carmel with his wife in 1914. He built a tower out of seaside granite and planted thousands of cypress and eucalyptus trees. When he died in 1962, much of his land had been sold off to pay taxes and sewer assessment fees required for financing the suburban specter Henry Miller had described. During that time, Jeffers had become more enamored of nature and less enamored of man.

Wasting the world on your own labor, without love
     possessing not even your hands to the dirt
     but plows
Like blades of knives; heartless machines; houses of
     steel: using and despising the patient earth . . .

The night-time glow of city lights reminded Jeffers of the glistening bodies of sardines hauled together in a purse-seine, and led to a pessimistic conclusion:

There is no escape. We have gathered vast populations
     incapable of free survival, insulated
From the strong earth, each person in himself helpless,
     on all dependent. The circle is closed, and the net
Is being hauled in . . .

Jeffers had made his escape from the urban net ("I have still a furlong of granite cliff, on which the Pacific leans his wild weight . . .") and he clung to it resolutely.

The county taxes take all my income, and it seems
   ridiculous
To hold three acres of shorelong woodland
And the little low house that my own hands made, at
   the annual cost
Of a shiny new car. Never mind, the trees and the
   stones are worth it.

Jeffers speaks of how the rest of the world might escape the net:

A little too abstract, a little too wise,
It is time for us to kiss the earth again . . .

Jeffers had little hope that mankind would accept his advice. Catastrophe seemed a more likely prospect. "Some day this coast will dip and be clean," was one of his forecasts. His tribulations as a property owner contributed to his pessimism. According to his biographer, Melba Bennett, the poet sent this protest against a sewer assessment to the Carmel *Pine Cone:*

As to our own place, it is ridiculous to assess us more than six thousand dollars . . . for a facility which we shall never need; while a big new house covering a little lot, which therefore perhaps really needs the service, will pay less than one hundred and fifty dollars—more than forty times less. But we shall not press this absurdity; but consider ourselves fortunate as long as we are not actually compelled to hook up with a system that at present shockingly defiles the rivermouth and may in future pollute the bay . . .

In another response to the pressures of growth, the town of Carmel planned to condemn property for a library and a park. Jeffers, the lover of books and open space, cut short a trip to Ireland to protest once again. His daughter-in-law, Mrs. Lee Jeffers, wrote of ". . . the dismal and heart-breaking reason for our almost immediate return—a master plan for Carmel—a map showing Tor House as a Memorial Library and Robin's land as a public park." According to the daughter-in-law, Jeffers the property owner now felt compelled to embrace the very kind of development he deplored as a poet.

The matter upset Robin dreadfully. He detested the thought of having the land tied up by zoning laws, etc., for many years with him paying taxes and not being able to sell if the necessity arose . . . as soon

as we returned Robin subdivided 10 of the lower lots into three large building sites and sold them, feeling if there were a few more houses and owners to contend with, the plan for a park would be less desirable . . . seeing the trees go down has been the hardest to bear . . .

In the midst of this dilemma, Jeffers wrote to one friend: "I don't think industrial civilization is worth the distortion of human nature, and the meanness and loss of contact with the earth that it entails. I think your Marxist industrialized communism—if it were ever brought into existence—would be only a further step in a bad direction."

Jeffers also wrote, "Some of you think you can save society. I think it is impossible, and that you (radicals, social uplifters, etc.) only hasten the process of decadence." In 1970, Monterey Bay served to confirm Jeffers' pessimism. With bay waters under swimming quarantine and scuba divers warned to take shots for hepatitis, a new rash of sewer bonds was floated to extend the sewer system.

Yet Jeffers may have underestimated the ability of the Pacific shore to bring forth noble as well as crass impulses. Long before Jeffers began eulogizing it, a visitor, Frederick Law Olmsted, was formulating a strategy to preserve and protect the landscape of California. During the Civil War, after setting up what later became the Red Cross, he had come there for a rest. On a trip along the coast Olmsted saw oil seeps as a potential bonanza: "If there is any oil to be gotten in this way, there will be enough to float all the navies of the world, etc. . . . I have got a good deal 'in oil' if it ever comes to anything." However, the amateur speculator was also a pioneer landscape architect, the creator of Central Park in New York City. To Olmsted, "the marked feature" on the coast was not oil seepage but the redwoods. The beauty and the vulnerability of the big California trees suggested to Olmsted what was still a relatively new concept: "The establishment by government of great public grounds for the free enjoyment of the people . . . is . . . justified and enforced as a political duty."

Although his own investment in oil seeps was premature, Olmsted's words inspired men like

Muir to nurture the national and state park systems. The exploitation of the Pacific shore dramatized the need for new concepts in earth management. The sheer grandeur of the redwood forests became a symbol of the need for protection. Silt and flooding as a result of careless mining and lumbering were a demonstration of the harm that came of ignoring natural values. In the words of Abbott Kinney, a Los Angeles reformer of the 1880s, "The pine tree sings in the Sierra a song that is echoed in the rich rustle of grain on the distant plain. Let us not forget that though so far apart, the interests of the plain are entwined with those of the mountain, and without forests we may also be without farms."

Ironically, Kinney did not bring these insights to the project of building a beach resort at Venice, near Los Angeles. A breakwater was installed to protect a pier; the result was an eroded beach. A slough was carved up into a labyrinth of canals, which ultimately became sluggish gutters. The perceptions of the artist, the scientist, and the reformer had not yet merged in a coherent whole.

In a fascinating paper entitled "Philosophy on Cannery Row" (included in *Steinbeck: The Man and His Work,* Oregon State University Press, 1971), the marine scientist Joel Hedgpeth suggests how the tide pools of the Pacific shore helped to bring together such perceptions. In 1923 John Steinbeck, then a Stanford University undergraduate, took a course in marine biology at Hopkins Marine Station in Pacific Grove. Professor Rolf Bolin of the Station later recalled:

I gained the impression that his Marine Station experience was a real eye-opener, but the only specific idea that he ever indicated to me as resulting from it was a concept of a group of individuals acting as a superorganism in the same way that an individual acts as a supercell. Although this idea is a keystone in modern ecology, it was fairly new then, I believe, and I was first struck by it in discussions with John.

Steinbeck's interest in marine biology led to an acquaintance with Edward Ricketts, who ran a marine specimen collecting service in the Monterey area, and who was later depicted as the fun-loving Doc in Steinbeck's *Cannery Row.* But Ricketts was more than a womanizer, drinker, and collector of barnacles. As a marine naturalist, he conceived and became coauthor, with Jack Calvin, of *Between Pacific Tides,* published in 1939. According to Hedgpeth, this was "the first book for general readers to discuss the distribution of animals on the seashore according to their levels of occurrence and to attempt to use this zonal distribution as an aid to identification." Moreover, like Steinbeck, Ricketts was struck by the philosophical concept of the superorganism.

Who would see a replica of man's social structure has only to examine the abundant and various life of the tidepools, where miniature communal societies wage dubious battle against equally potent societies in which the individual is paramount, with trans-shifting, maturing, or dying out, with all the living organisms balanced against the limitations of the dead kingdom of rocks and currents and temperatures and dissolved gases.

In 1940 Steinbeck and Ricketts went on a collecting expedition to the Gulf of California. The result was a book, *Sea of Cortez,* which at first received little attention, since its release coincided with the Japanese attack on Pearl Harbor. An abridged later version, *The Log from the Sea of Cortez,* listed Steinbeck as sole author, although Ricketts' contribution was substantial. It was here that the two men described the frenetic exploitation of a local shrimp fishery by the Japanese as "a true crime against nature and against the immediate welfare of Mexico and the eventual welfare of the human species," and reaffirmed the necessity for standing with, rather than apart from, the physical environment:

. . . man is related to the whole thing, related inextricably to all reality, known and unknowable. That is a simple thing to say, but the profound feeling of it made a Jesus, a St. Augustine, a St. Francis, a Roger Bacon, a Charles Darwin, and an Einstein. Each . . . reaffirmed with astonishment the knowledge that all things are one thing and that one thing is all things—plankton, a shimmering phosphorescence on the sea, and the spinning planets and an expanding universe, all bound together by the elastic string of time. *It is advisable to look from the tide pool to the stars and then back to the tide pool again.*

In their own time, admirers of the Pacific shore from Dana to Ricketts and Steinbeck were considered worthy of attention as literary men but were not taken seriously as philosophers, educators, or civic leaders. Yet their warnings have been fulfilled a hundred times over. Dana, Stevenson, and Kipling recognized that there was much more to the Pacific shore than a series of bonanzas. Muir and Greeley warned of how easily the values of the shore, tangible and intangible, could be destroyed. Jeffers declared that in destroying these values we were deforming our own existence. Jack London foresaw the retribution that was in store for the Pacific coast: today the Corps of Engineers spends millions of dollars to clear San Francisco Bay of such navigational hazards as the sunken pilings that London encountered half a century ago, and to dredge up the silt that still flows from the denuded mountain slopes noted with such dismay by Greeley. Kinney, Olmsted, Ricketts and Steinbeck all wrote of the need to enlarge our perspectives.

The voices of these men, unheeded as prophets in their own time, are far more audible today. The satire that Browne employed over a century ago is continued by the San Francisco poet Lawrence Ferlinghetti: "I see where Walden Pond has been drained/ to make an amusement park."

The lonely rebellion of a Jeffers or a Max Miller is transformed into public protest. The folksinger Malvina Reynolds sings in defense of "The Fragile Sea":

Our source, our provider and our road to liberty,
Now we use it as a dump hole for this mad economy,
And we never will survive a dying sea.

Such concerns extend into academic circles as well. Dr. Paul Rudy, an ichthyologist who came to Coos Bay, Oregon, to direct the University of Oregon's Institute of Marine Biology, found his research complicated by dredges, outfalls and land fills: "When I moved to the Coos Bay region it soon became apparent to me that I was observing the destruction of an estuary. The physiological studies and salt water balance didn't seem very important when the environment that justified the organism's existence was disappearing." Today Dr. Rudy devotes part of his time to testifying in defense of the estuary before city councils and state agencies. A growing number of people along the Pacific shore are no longer willing to adapt to a narrowed existence and a crippled environment. Thus the concern of those who celebrated it in the past still lives on by the Pacific shore.

Chapter 7

Return of the Near-Exterminated

From the air, San Miguel Island looks like a large sand dune wedged between the light blue of the sky and the dark blue of the Pacific. A mere shiver of landscape, it would seem to exist at the whim of the sea; one big wave might be the end of it.

The island lies about an hour away from the freeway snarls and bulkheaded shores of Los Angeles. But no autos honk here. There are no roads and no gutters. Sea breezes and waves run free, undeterred by breakwaters or construction of any kind.

You can stand alone on San Miguel, the sea breezes tugging at your clothes, the surf thundering in your ears, Los Angeles seeming as far away as the moon—and still you don't feel alone. The abalone shells strewn about the island are a reminder that here the Chumash once lived and died, and gathered in their sociable temescals. Grasslands, laid waste by sheep that grazed here a century ago, are now attempting to recolonize the sandy dunes. As sand and grass struggle for control of the landscape, a ranch house built of shipwrecked timbers slowly crumbles. Here a World War I veteran, a victim of nerve gas, lived with his family until World War II. Then the Navy needed the island as a punching bag for ship salvos, and the family were ordered to evacuate to Santa Barbara. They did . . . except for the World War I veteran. An apparent suicide, he lies buried near the site of a little schoolhouse he built for his two children.

This island harbors more than just memories and echoes. Above the crashing combers you can hear a dull roar, as though from a remote football stadium. If you hike across the island towards the sound, you reach a bluff overlooking a sand spit. Sea lions crowd the spit, sunning themselves. In their midst lie the mammoth, almost shapeless forms of the elephant seal, which was once believed to have been exterminated by harpoon and bullet. But there they are, their prowess as marine animals reduced to a snaillike sluggishness on land. As one wrenches towards the surf, suddenly the 8000-pound bulk becomes a sleek, torpedolike form able to hunt down squid and sharks.

In 1892, fewer than one hundred northern elephant seals clustered on Guadalupe Island, another sliver of land that lies off Baja California. As the gunfire died away and the harpoons no longer struck, this remnant herd began to spread out and reclaim ancestral rookeries hundreds of miles away. By 1950, there were perhaps fifty elephant seals on San Miguel; by 1952 there were 412; today there are over 3000. Other species have returned from the brink—the Guadalupe fur seal and the Alaska fur seal. San Miguel Island, though not far from freeways and smog alerts, has become a principal stage for one of the most remarkable comebacks in the annals of wildlife conservation. No aquarium on the mainland can match the magnificence of this sanctuary for the nearly exterminated. The island is vibrant with the squeal of seabirds and the cadence of the surf, but above all it is the roar of its resurgent seal colonies that a visitor remembers.

One turns hopefully from the sand spit to the kelp forests offshore, looking eagerly for a small furry form that floats on its back, wrapped in a kelp frond, patiently working to crack a mussel shell with a rock. No sea otters are to be seen here. But if you go further north, to the Big Sur area that Jeffers eulogized, to where Ed Ricketts stalked the rocky shore in hip boots, to where Robert Louis Stevenson, coughing and ill, could still rhapsodize over the beauty of the enveloping fog, you may see a thing they were never privileged to view: sea otters by the hundreds. It may well be that one day the sea otter will also return to San Miguel.

In Oregon, where there is no remnant herd, those eager to restore the sea otter have found a strange technological ally. Recently, the otters on one Aleutian island had to be evacuated because of impending underground nuclear tests. Transferred to other Alaskan rookeries, these exiles might have upset the balance in the existing populations. So the state of Oregon joined an airlift that brought the displaced mammals to its own waters. Although they appear to be doing well, it is too early to tell whether they will be able to reproduce successfully. In 1974, four years after the airlift, there was a small but stable population of between twenty-two and twenty-four otters, including three immature animals and four pups. "It is encouraging of course to see the animals reproducing so well, but the numbers are so few that I consider the population to be 'walking a survival tight-rope,'" observes Bruce Mate of the Environmental Health Services Center at Oregon State University, a principal member of the "transplant" team.

Nor does this complete the roll call of the near-exterminated. Some years ago, outside the beachfront apartment where the ocean upset our beach party, I saw what looked like a small fountain periodically spouting in the Pacific. After observing three or four more such spouts, I realized that I had been looking at my first whale. What I didn't realize was that this was a gray whale, another mammal returned from the brink. At the time, I had never expected to see a whale off any shore, least of all southern California. I had thought all whales—or whatever was left of them—frequented the open ocean. Nothing in my education or my boyhood days at the beach had taught me to look for whales spouting within sight of my window. My father, a native and lifelong resident of California, had never even seen one. Only after consulting a library and talking with scientists at Scripps Institution of Oceanography did I realize I had been witnessing another comeback along the coast. I did not fully appreciate the impact of the gray whale's return till I landed in a dirt runway halfway down the narrow desert peninsula of Baja California. After a short, bumpy car ride, I looked over the lagoon where Scammon had come across the gray whale herd, and where he and his whaling cohorts had struck their big bonanza. There were no harpooners trading curses over tangled lines, no huge metal vats boiling whale blubber. But there were fountain spouts by the hundreds. Indeed, they were so profuse as to suggest the notion that the desert lagoon had an underwater sprinkling system.

Scammon had expressed concern about the survival of the gray whale before the turn of the century. In the 1930s, one naturalist in the San Diego area estimated that out of a pre-whaling population of 30,000, "no more than a few dozen" any longer existed. Today, an estimated 9000 gray whales commute between their summer feeding grounds in the Arctic and their winter calving grounds in the desert lagoons of Baja California.

It would be pleasant to think that all of these creatures made it back entirely on their own. But it happens not to be true. One thing did contribute significantly to their survival: scientists estimate that 4 percent of the bulls in a sea elephant herd may be able to inseminate 84 percent of the females. This reservoir of sexual potency makes the comeback of the elephant seals easier to understand. But they still needed help from the species that almost exterminated them. The gray whales were among the first—and almost accidental—beneficiaries of legislative restraints on the exploitation of resources that writers such as Greeley and Stevenson had warned against. By the time those laws were enacted, there were few whalers or seal hunters left to lobby against or even to break them.

In 1913, when the first ban on killing sea otters was enacted in California, there was considerable doubt whether any otters still remained. Most of the legislators who supported this ban were dead by the time the otters' comeback was publicly confirmed in 1938. A ban on hunting elephant seals was considered even more futile. Fortunately, Mexico enacted such a ban after the remnant herd at Guadalupe Island was discovered in 1907. The killing of gray whales was prohibited by international accord in 1938 when it was discovered that some still remained to be protected.

The protected marine mammals that have survived now face new and more insidious threats. Oil from the blowout in the Santa Barbara Channel washed ashore at San Miguel, and there were reports that sea lion pups had been killed. An investigation verified that sea lions had indeed been coated with oil and that some pups were dead, but no conclusive link was found. If the spill had occurred earlier in the pupping season, when the females were nursing, and their teats had been exposed to oil, the pups might have ingested milk liberally mixed with Santa Barbara crude. This could have been deadly.

A number of dead pups, both with and without oil on their coats, were observed to have been born prematurely. Up to 20 percent of the pups in the herd had been premature. Some mothers were seen attempting to revive the aborted pups by dragging them into the surf. Reports of premature pupping aroused the interest of a biochemist, Robert Risebrough of the University of California at Berkeley, who is among those who believe there is a link between the occurrence of brittle eggshells in seabirds and their intake of DDT. Subsequent tests showed that California sea lions had higher DDT residues than any other marine mammal yet examined. Aborting females showed much higher pesticide counts than nonaborting females. Dr. Risebrough believes the intake of DDT may upset the sea lion's hormone balance and induce premature pupping. Although his contention is disputed by some scientists, another piece of circumstantial

evidence has come to light. Recently, the Montrose Chemical Corporation stopped dumping DDT wastes into Los Angeles' ocean outfall system. Subsequently, Dr. Robert DeLong of the University of California at Berkeley found pesticide levels in the sea lions at San Miguel Island to be decreasing. Dr. DeLong also reports an apparent decrease in premature pupping. Elephant seals manage to avoid such potentially lethal additives because of a difference in diet: they feed on sharks, rays, and other deep-water creatures that don't accumulate as much DDT as do anchovies, mackerel, and other surface feeders that are preferred by sea lions.

The sea otter must contend with similar threats. If and when an oil spill occurs off central California, the otter's comeback may be impeded. A coat of oil on the fur of the otter may rob it of insulation in the cold waters and expose it to pneumonia.

The otter must also contend with those who consider its comeback an "economic menace." Spokesmen for the commercial abalone industry contend that sea otters deplete abalone stocks—and to back up this contention, abalone divers display photos of otters retrieving abalone and feeding on the creamy meat. As a result of this unpardonable competition, the otter's appetite becomes "voracious." Otter herds are depicted as "trampling" and "devastating" abalone beds. The proposed solution: remove the otters.

Although the gray whale no longer has to contend with harpoons in its calving grounds, it does face the problem of tourism and industrial development. Great barges that serve a salt works continually cross Scammon Lagoon. During calving time, sightseeing boats that descended upon the lagoon have been known to chase down whales for a "good look."

Thus, the near-exterminated still need defenders . . . and they have come forth. Richard Boolootian, a zoologist at the University of California at Los Angeles, has helped debunk the charge that the otter is an economic menace. The otter's principal diet happens to be sea urchins—not abalone, which were actually more abundant when otters frolicked by the hundreds of thousands along the California coast. Today, with no more than a thousand otters, the abalone is far less abundant, particularly in the rocky intertidal area. What accounts for this? The Friends of the Sea Otter suggest that the abalone industry itself is the main threat to the stocks of abalone. To date, the state legislature has resisted the pleas of the abalone industry to evict the "voracious" otters. At the same time, the legislature is considering more stringent regulations on the voracity of sportsmen and commercial divers.

Encouraged by conservationists and by scientists such as Dr. Carl Hubbs of the Scripps Institution of Oceanography, the government of Mexico has imposed restrictions on boat traffic in Scammon Lagoon and classified it as a sanctuary to protect the gray whale. Mexico's actions on behalf of both the gray whale and the elephant seal belie the contention that developing nations can't afford—or prefer to ignore—wildlife resources.

At the urging of Dr. Hubbs and the Santa Barbara chapter of the Sierra Club, the National Park Service now administers San Miguel as a sanctuary for seals. Besides protecting them, the Park Service is helping the native plants to reclaim the island landscape from the sand.

The decision of the Montrose Chemical Corporation to stop draining DDT (600 pounds daily, according to the Los Angeles County Sanitation District) into the Pacific Ocean may have been spurred by a lawsuit brought by the Environmental Defense Fund and based on the work of Dr. Risebrough and Dr. DeLong.

The comeback of these marine mammals is a cultural event not only for conservationists but for the public in general. Thousands drive along the central California coast to catch a glimpse of the sea otter herds. As in the days of the Makah and Nootka Indians, the migration of the gray whale stimulates something like a ritual up and down the coast. Charter boats and planes offer the public a close-up view of the whales. Students and teachers turn their attention to the whale in the classroom and then go to the nearest bluff to observe it at first hand. The American Cetacean Society uses the Goodyear blimp to conduct a yearly census of gray whales. One of the most heavily visited of the areas administered by the National Park Service, Cabrillo National Monument in San Diego, is popular mainly because it overlooks the whale migration. The public pays a total of $70,000 each year to view the gray whale from plane, blimp, or boat up and down the coast.

The comeback of the marine mammals has become a scientific boon too. The gray whale's accessibility in desert lagoons makes it a favorite target for scientists seeking to understand the physiology of the world's largest living creature. Scientists study the elephant seal's ability to swallow food under water without taking water into its lungs, to conserve its body heat in water at 50° F. and to submerge for intervals of from 20 to 40 minutes between breaths at the surface.

The sea otter may become an important working partner with scientists. Its fondness for urchins made it a principal control on urchin populations in pre-harpooning days. Scientists are now considering moving some sea otters from central California to feed on urchin-infested kelp forests in southern California.

These marine mammals are thus proving more valuable alive than killed and skinned. Yet their comeback may have even greater significance in that they cannot function apart from their environment. Thus, citizens and public officials concerned with protecting these mammals have had to ensure protection of the entire marine environment.

As our own population needs place ever greater stress on the capacity of the planet to support it, such a partnership with nature becomes important to our own survival. For example, the levels of DDT that affect the mammals have caused the Food and Drug Administration to take certain kinds of fish off the commercial market. A healthy marine environment will also be important to other nearly depleted species that manage to return. As a result of the ban on sardine fishing, fishery officials anticipate that the sardine population will eventually support a commercial fishery . . . though not until the end of the century. (Some scientists are concerned that the population of a competitor species—the anchovy—has expanded to take over the sardine's ecological niche.) The comeback of this particular species, although not as picturesque as the whale, may prove quite as important. When the sardine bonanza was at its height, the nation was in the middle of the Depression. In those bleak days, canned sardines were a cheap but wholesome source of protein for millions without refrigerators. Given the increasing global competition for protein, the sardine's comeback by the year 2000 may prove most timely . . . but not if it triggers another race towards depletion.

These successes in bringing back the near-exterminated have had a particular effect on me. The unpredictable nature of the Malibu beach near my apartment made me aware of the critical interplay that sustains the Pacific shore. Although I found it fascinating, it did not enter my mind that this interplay could be a subject to write about. At the time I was writing about the social and political impact of the aerospace industry. This seemed to have more pertinence, since I still saw the ocean as another "hostile" environment in which aerospace technology could prove itself. But as I began to observe the consequences of treating the shore as a jumbo resource—the eroded beaches, the shrinking estuaries, the "NO TRESPASSING" signs—I became more and more concerned about the future of the Pacific shore. Were we fore-doomed to despoil the ocean as we had despoiled the land? It was with such forebodings that I traveled to Scammon Lagoon where I watched as gray whales cleared the lagoon surface, upending momentarily and then subsiding into the water with an explosion of foam. Such "spyhopping" served as eloquent testimony not only to the whale's agility, but to the perceptiveness of those who, long before Earth Days, environmental impact statements, and commercialized whale watching, saw the need for political action to protect rather than exploit the Pacific shore.

Chapter 8

No Longer Real Estate

The scenic Oregon coast is not only a natural but also a social marvel—the greatest single expanse of publicly controlled seashore in the United States. It is difficult to predict what other shorelines will look like twenty or thirty years from now. But one can predict, with some degree of confidence, that in Oregon much of it will be as open and beautiful as it still is today—and as it was a century ago.

That Oregon has achieved this distinction is surprising. Although the Oregon shore is exceptionally beautiful, with its rocky flanks marching out into the Pacific, because of its chilly waters and strong nearshore currents it is not particularly inviting to swimmers. As the westernmost point of the Pacific shore, it receives the full brunt of ocean combers. It is a popular recreation simply to watch storm waves explode against the rocks in tremendous, geyserlike bursts of surf.

Yet this ruggedness has tended to rebuff the pressure of development, which has brought urbanization to other coasts. In sharp contrast to that of southern California, Oregon's population is mainly concentrated inland, around the gentle Willamette Valley.

The Oregon shore has never lacked would-be developers. If they had their way, it would already be dropping out of view behind electronic gates, high-rise buildings, and other scenic blockbusters. Its rocky headlands would be mere viewsites, its beach strands a series of narrow lots, and its dunes "borrow pits" for construction fill. But while other states have eagerly given away the natural heritage of their shorelines, Oregon has determinedly sought to hold and add to this heritage.

This is by no means a new concept. The Roman Code of Justinian I declared that by natural right "the air, running water, the sea, and consequently the seashore" were "common to all."

> No one therefore is forbidden access to the seashore, provided he abstains from injury to [improvements] . . . The public use of the seashore, as of the sea itself, is part of the law of nations; consequently, every one is free to build a cottage upon it for purposes of retreat [recreation], as well as to dry his nets and haul them up from the sea. But they cannot be said to belong to anyone as private property, but rather are subject to the same law as the sea itself, with the soil or sand that lies beneath it.

English common law asserted public ownership from the mean high tide line seaward, and this doctrine was carried over to the United States. The common law similarly recognized the need to release tidelands for navigation and for shore-related reclamation and improvement projects. In the United States, public agencies can dispose of tidelands and submerged lands, subject to public navigation and fishing rights. This regulation often becomes a loophole, permitting states to auction off public tidelands as if they were surplus military property. State legislatures and city councils beguiled by property tax revenues have not hesitated to alienate tidelands for private purposes, shore-related or otherwise. Public easements for navigation and fisheries become obscured by six feet of earth fill. A vertical concrete shore can make public ownership up to the mean high tide line rather academic, unless you happen to be a barnacle. One overlooked fact of nature along the Pacific shore favors exclusive development: whereas the twice-daily high tides on the English coast and on our Atlantic coast generally reach about the same elevation, along the Pacific there are a high-high tide and a high-low tide, reflecting a notable difference in elevation. The mean high tide is thus actually below the highest high tide at least 20 percent of the time. As Dr. Joel Hedgpeth observes in *Between Pacific Tides*, "The effect of this is to establish property rights to tidelands property at lower levels than those on the Atlantic coast, and to prevent access to the shore even more . . . One may, of course, take consolation in the thought that in the fullness of time (or sooner, if the greenhouse effect melts the glaciers) the sea will rise again and wash away all the private estates, fancy motels, and condominiums—as well as all the marine laboratories."

In the late eighteenth and early nineteenth centuries, the Oregon legislature, like those of other states, was recklessly peeling off state tidelands at the behest of salmon entrepreneurs in quest of exclusive seining grounds, and of railroad magnates in quest of convenient shoreline rights of way. This did not sit too well with a state land agent, Oswald West. Instead of getting in on the tideland rush, he became a reform governor. Aware that government itself, as well as developers, must be restrained if indiscriminate tideland development is to be prevented, West moved cautiously. "I knew," he wrote, "that any proposed measure to withdraw the beaches from sale would attract the attention of the land owners and the legislatures would be swamped with protests and the state land board with applications to purchase the lands."

The natural character of the Oregon shore came to West's rescue. The steep verticals of the coastal range made travel difficult. The beaches, often the only level area along the coast, became impromptu roads. Rather unobtrusively, West submitted a bill declaring the seashore between the Washington and California state lines a public highway. "I pointed out that thus we would come into miles and miles of highway without cost to the taxpayer." The legislature, anxious to build but not to finance roads, approved.

West's bill did not give the public anything it already didn't own, but it lessened the temptation to alienate the seashore. Free from economic speculation, coastal lands could be acquired for public use at reasonable prices. While other states auctioned off their coastal heritage, Oregon was acquiring a chain of fine coastal parks embracing sandy beaches, dune fields, the rocky shore, and coastal bluffs.

It is thanks to such foresight that a major part of Oregon coast is publicly owned. (Of suitable recreational land along the Atlantic and the Gulf of Mexico, over 90 percent is in private hands.) Approximately 112 miles did remain private, and the temptation to fence off access and claim exclusive use also remained. By the mid-1960s, log barriers and fences began cropping up along the Oregon shore. In the words of one motel owner, "It is my intention to have the nicest ocean front in this state, and that means keeping a private beach area for my guests."

One such closure of the open shore may appear insignificant; yet it portends a relentless alteration of the shore's social character. Once open to all as a natural resource, it becomes a commodity to be enjoyed by a few. Who qualifies to enjoy it? "One who wants privacy, a large lot, plenty of inner space, and that illusive quality best described as character," declares a coastal developer who describes himself as "The Great Character Builder." There is also one other requirement: the ability to purchase a $100,000 house. Having fulfilled this requirement, one can enter a seaside kingdom and enjoy "nothing but the sky above you and the blue sea beyond." The inspiration and refreshment that Dana and Stevenson once took from the Pacific, free, now come with big price tags: "Visual masterpiece of rare waterfront elegance" or "Epitome of luxurious on-the-water living." The Great Character Builder has even appropriated one of Stevenson's fictional settings—Spyglass Hill—for the coastal slope he has carved into estates.

On the exclusive shore, such simple objects as fish poles, surfboards, and sand-castle molds become passé, superseded by marble pullmans, skylighted atriums and subterranean garages. "Electronic entrance gates and an intercom system for total security" keep the outside world at bay.

The shift from democracy to exclusiveness is not confined to "undeveloped" or "empty" shores. Older beach neighborhoods that accommodate the young, the elderly, and families of moderate means, and which have never needed electronic gates, can also be victimized. They can be taxed out of existence by the same inexorable forces of growth that crowded Jeffers on his "furlong of granite cliff, on which the Pacific leans his wild weight." The Miami Towers and the Spyglass Hills take over and keep the shore safe for moneyed Character.

This dramatic shift in the social character of the shore is often justified by alleging a need to protect the shore from the public. Why should the American shore be protected from Americans, and a price tag placed on sunsets and ocean-washed sand? Because public access is seen as an invitation to garbage dumping, littering, and vandalism. In Florida, one developer even managed to close off a shore street-end easement on the basis that its popularity with love-making couples endangered public morals. In southern California, a Marine general said, criticizing a proposal by Congressman Alphonzo Bell to open a portion of Camp Pendleton's seventeen-mile-long barbed-wire beachfront to the public: "This clown says 'turn it over to the hippies, because the Marines aren't using it.' That beach has a capacity for a thousand people. But what kind of people? One thousand hippies or people we can trust?" President Nixon intervened to ensure that the public could share this beachfront without enlisting in the Marine Corps or getting a crew cut.

Public abuse is certainly as legitimate a concern as private abuse. However, it has often been invoked as a reason for closing off access to beaches instead of seeking ways of sharing use and maintenance. To protect public beaches from the "outside" public, some city councils have refrained from building adequate restroom facilities. This imposed bladder control inspired a piece of anonymous verse.

"No restrooms for the peasants!" . . . A powerful call
By privileged rich with homes along the Wall.
They ignore the plight of an embarrassed child
And turn their heads at the stink so wild.

Here at Longfellow, we cry for a public head,
But you'll landscape the RR tracks instead.

To a blind council, I dedicate this old salute,
(Then return to the ocean to again pollute):

Oh why, of all the things that had to be
Must we, at Longfellow, have no place to pee?

If a public agency continues to insist on public access to a beach despite the alleged shortcomings of the human race, a private beach owner may offer his alternative to shared access—public purchase of his uplands. In urban coastal states where beachfront values are spiraling, the owner offers this alternative secure in the knowledge that the state will eventually bankrupt itself. The "Public-is-a-pig" argument and the specter of purchase have persuaded many state legislatures to tolerate gradual closure of the beachfront. A large segment of the Oregon public, however, was not willing to tolerate this. Millions of inland Oregon residents had become accustomed to going to the beach crossing the uplands on their way. That this traditional access could be summarily wiped out by barbed wire seemed unfair. Was the shore to be treated as an ordinary piece of real estate? And would those fences be succeeded by high-rise apartments and franchised restaurants? Must the Oregon shore, despite farsighted acquisitions, become an urbanized copy of the others? There was mounting public pressure on the legislature for control over the use of dry as well as wet sands to preclude such a fate. But how could that control be put into effect without disrupting existing property development? Years of public passage over private uplands can result in a prescriptive public right to use these uplands. As Willis West, a deputy district attorney and nephew of the late Governor West, observed:

> The acts of 1899 and 1913 dedicating the ocean beaches between ordinary high and low tides as a public highway not only established an eastern right-of-way line for public use and travel, but laid a legal basis for the acquisition of the dry sand area eastward through prescriptive uses. Wagons, automobiles, saddle horses, foot travelers, and a multitude of parents and plain children have finished the job.

The highway department made a survey and reported that, of 112 miles of private dry sand beach, sixty miles received moderate to heavy use, the remainder light use. A legislative bill gave the highway commission permit powers over fences or any other structures built on dry sands. Concerned members of the Oregon State University Oceanographic faculty, including Dr. Hedgpeth and Dr. Jeff Goner, provided expert advice free of charge on proper beach definitions. The bill was designed "to forever preserve and maintain the sovereignty of the state heretofore existing over the seashore and ocean beaches of the state . . ." It was challenged in the courts as taking private property without just compensation. However, in a test case, Appellate Judge J. S. Bohannon pointed out that beachfront cannot be considered as ordinary real estate without doing injustice to the overriding interests of society. "Oregon beaches are in a class by themselves, distinguishable from all other classes of property . . . In reality, the only utility of a beach is recreation. This fact has been the reason that commercial establishments such as defendants' motel have been constructed on the edge of the beach . . ." The judge noted evidence that the public had used the beach in question for more than half a century and "that public funds were expended on the beach for the removal of logs, for providing police protection, for providing traffic control, and for providing lifeguard service." The judge thereupon upheld the validity of public prescriptive rights.

The courts of other states, including California, have recently upheld public prescriptive rights in specific instances. The Oregon bill, however, raised the issue of control over the entire beachfront of the state. In reviewing the test case on appeal, the Oregon Supreme Court turned to the law of customary rights. Steve McKeon, writing on "Beach Access" for the *Stanford Law Review*, pointed out:

> The law of customary rights arose in medieval England. Inhabitants of many feudal villages had received manorial privileges and rights in the private property of their feudal lord long before England had any formal system for recording or otherwise recognizing these property interests. The doctrine of custom grew out of the feeling that a usage which had lasted for centuries must surely have been founded upon a legal right conferred at some time in the dim past. The holders of the right were not penalized because no formal recording system existed when they first received it. Custom was recognized as a valid source of law.

The court noted the argument by the private beach developers "that because of the relative brevity of our political history it is inappropriate to rely upon an English doctrine that requires greater antiquity than a newly settled land can claim." However, the court noted, "The first European settlers on these shores found the aboriginal inhabitants using the fore shore for clam digging and the dry sand area for their cooking fires. The newcomers continued these customs after statehood." Ironically, the coastal Indians had come to the rescue of the palefaces even though few of the former were left to enjoy the fruits of customary use.

The iconoclastic determination of Oregon to keep the shore public and open reverberated across the continent. A headline in the Miami Beach (Florida) *Times* declared, "Landmark Decision by Oregon Court Would Remove Hotel Barriers." Hotels in Miami Beach have been allowed to restrict beach access to hotel clientele. Street-end easements become ornate hotel lobby entrances. Private beach recreation facilities, such as swimming pools, have literally buried the beach and hastened erosion. Hotel owners resisted a federal project to replenish the twenty-mile-long beach because use of public funds would require that the restored beach be public. Inspired by the Oregon decision, Mayor Jay Dermer of Miami Beach renewed his drive to secure more access, declaring, "The beaches, all sand, earth and ground, really belong to the public." In 1973 the Miami Beach hotel owners assented to the beach restoration project. Competitive pressures from a Disneyland development upcoast had helped overcome their distaste for public access.

According to the *Yale Law Journal,* "We are witnessing a sharp acceleration of a process begun around the time of Magna Charta, the reclamation of the public's interest in the fore shore. Perhaps the day when common law citizens will have as many rights in the fore shore as Roman citizens once did is near at hand."

To hasten that day, Congressman Robert Eckhardt of Texas has proposed a National Open Beaches Act "to prohibit the erection of barriers which interfere with public ingress and egress of public lands." Eckhardt notes that, in sharp contrast to Oregon, only 4 percent of the nation's 84,240 miles of shore are available for public recreation.

For many parts of the urban coastline, unfortunately, customary use has been exclusive use. The principle of shared public use has had to be won over and over again. Near where I live in southern California, a modest public easement manages to penetrate an exclusive coastal development flanked by electric gates and ornate guardhouses. Behind this easement lies a political and legal battle. The easement leads to Salt Creek beach, whose natural beauty and fine surfing waves have attracted board surfers, skin divers, and artists for many years. One day the surfers and artists found their access blocked by a chain. Another beach had apparently been lost to the public. The Orange County Board of Supervisors, to which people turned in protest, was the same public agency that had granted a shore road easement to a developer. The protesters then turned to a local lawyer, William Wilcoxen, and an extensive citizens' campaign began. It generated considerable support, for the citizens had become increasingly sensitive to the loss of precious beachfront. The chagrined supervisors realized that they could no longer regard the shorefront as ordinary real estate.

Once the supervisors decided to respond to the citizen protest, they found considerable latent powers at their disposal. Public prescriptive rights were invoked to regain access to Salt Creek beach. A countywide survey of existing public access easements revealed that many had been camouflaged by lush vegetation and "NO PARKING" signs put up by private beach owners. A local public harbor agency next door to a public beach was even guilty of planned obscurity. The supervisors ordered the disguises removed and access signs posted. New coastal development is required to provide public access to the shore.

While helping engineer this renaissance in beach access, Wilcoxen found himself being literally outflanked on the beaches of his home city. A slate of candidates who campaigned hard on the issue of controlling hippies now controlled the city council of scenic Laguna Beach. Once in office, the new councilmen seemed to have lost interest in hippies but appeared entranced by visions of extensive high-rise development. Residents began to wonder if they had elected councilmen dedicated to obliterating public views of the beach. Were they in fact would-be architects of Miami Beach West? To forestall the possibility, a local group, Village Laguna, initiated a referendum on limiting high-rises. When legal action was taken to enjoin the referendum, Wilcoxen managed at the last moment to have the injunction lifted by an appellate court. The referendum passed by a large majority. The city councilmen who had camouflaged their plans for high-rise apartments with talk of hippie abatement found themselves earnestly reviewing recommendations by Village Laguna for a ceiling on population and community growth. A new council majority, led by Mayor Roy Holm, a Friends of the Earth member, has since displaced the high-rise advocates.

Oregon's magnificent achievement in shore protection requires no less in the way of continued vigilance. Commercial high-rise complexes sprout first along the coastal highway. Controls on these scenic blockbusters will be essential if the Oregon shore is to be seen as well as used.

The sandy shore, with its capacity for heavy

recreational use, is unique among outdoor areas. No forest floor or valley plain can so easily shrug off the imprints of a million feet. However, public access to the rocky shore, if uncontrolled, can be disastrous. Careless collecting can leave ghost tide pools where marine life once flourished. Collectors for the specialty restaurant trade have dropped copper sulfate crystals, nicotine, and other drugs into tide pools to daze octopus—a shortcut that can trigger massive tidal kills. Even science classes have resorted to using teardrops of nicotine to make collecting easier. Oregon has now established a chain of rocky shore preserves and instituted educational programs to save this habitat from such deadly enthusiasm. In southern California, Corona del Mar, a favorite with Ed Ricketts, is a tidepool preserve.

It is unfortunate that Jeffers, Muir, and Greeley cannot see the Oregon shore today. If they could, their faith in man's ability to exercise self-restraint might be somewhat restored. As with the gray whale and the otter, a substantial appreciation of the Pacific shore is beginning to supplant the Big Bonanza psychology. The natural values of free-flowing waves, public access to beaches and living tide pools are coming to be prized more than endless bulkheads, jetties, electronic guard gates, and other man-made improvements.

Such appreciation can in fact win out over the alleged economic attractions of the Big Bonanza psychology. In Oregon, forestalling intensive beach development has also precluded the costly side of intensive development. Much of the Oregon shore can be maintained both biologically and physically by natural processes that do not require massive programs for shoring up beach and bluff. Instead of relying on expensive public works, the Oregon shore will refresh the human spirit in a manner that no Disneyland can ever hope to duplicate . . . and at a price that the man in the street, and not only the man in the luxury residential marina, can afford.

A unique set of circumstances—the ruggedness of the Oregon coast, the foresight of Oswald West, the determination of an aroused beachgoing public —have gone into this example. It is one that could be lost rather quickly, given the eternal human temptation to exploit. The Big Bonanza psychology dies hard. Like a starfish with an injured limb, it has remarkable regenerative powers. Stop a high-rise developer on one shore and he crops up with an option on another. I recall visiting Ocean City, Maryland, where new high-rise buildings cast long afternoon shadows into the Atlantic. The scene suggested a congress of dinosaurs enjoying their last fling at immortality. Developers exiled from Florida by building restrictions eagerly touted their offerings to the Maryland shorescape via billboards and in breathless spot commercials on the radio. One building site, ringed with flags, carried the name of a developer from California who, when I last heard of him, had been vainly suing a group of environmentalists for blocking one of his pet reclamation schemes. But you must understand that this developer wasn't against ecology *per se*. You had only to look at the emblem on his fluttering flags: it was the *ecology* symbol, planted firmly in his reclaimed wetlands. Another trait of the Big Bonanza psychology is its ability to metamorphose into the most unlikely guises.

BEHIND THE SHORE

The Olympic Peninsula, especially the rain forest on its west side, warmed by the North Pacific current, is the most diverse and scenic landscape behind the shore. One of the United States' finest remaining coastal forests, the hemlock stand on the Peninsula's Third Beach, survives in its pristine, wild beauty only one hundred yards from the surf.

(right) Ancient coastal redwoods, clustered near Eureka, in northern California, are now protected by the National Park Service. This could be a mixed blessing if park "improvements" in the form of roads and accommodations should follow.

Bigleaf maple, Palo Colorado Canyon, Big Sur. The seasons pass easily along the west coast. Fall is marked only by less foggy, colder days than summer and the coloring of a few leaves, most conspicuously the bigleaf maple, companion tree of redwoods wherever they are found.

(right) Alder grove, Hoh Valley, Olympic Peninsula.

(left) Mosses and five-finger ferns, Fern Canyon, Redwoods National Park.

Hemlock Forest at Third Beach, Olympic Peninsula. Perhaps the Pacific Ocean's most profound influence on our land is reflected in the coastal forests of the Pacific Northwest. They are the finest and most prolific on earth. Sitka spruce, Douglas fir, western red cedar (canoe cedar) and western hemlock all grow to sizes found nowhere else.

Wind-pruned shrubbery, Ponsler, Oregon.

(right) Lace-lichens on live oaks, Santa Lucia Mountains, Big Sur. The oak is often regarded as the most typical tree of central California. Here, in the mountainous Big Sur region, they grow differently than in the broad valleys from Paso Robles to Los Angeles, with long, rambling limbs. Where fogs penetrate inland from the coast, the lace-lichen is apt to festoon anything that hangs in the air.

(left) Low tide, Tijuana Slough, California. Tijuana Slough is almost the only remaining slough in southern California. At one time there were several such small estuaries along the southern California coast: their meandering channels and mudflats are essential spawning grounds for the California halibut and habitat for resident and migratory shorebirds—herons and egrets, godwits, avocets and terns.

Pond, Point Reyes, California.

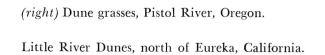

(right) Dune grasses, Pistol River, Oregon.

Little River Dunes, north of Eureka, California.

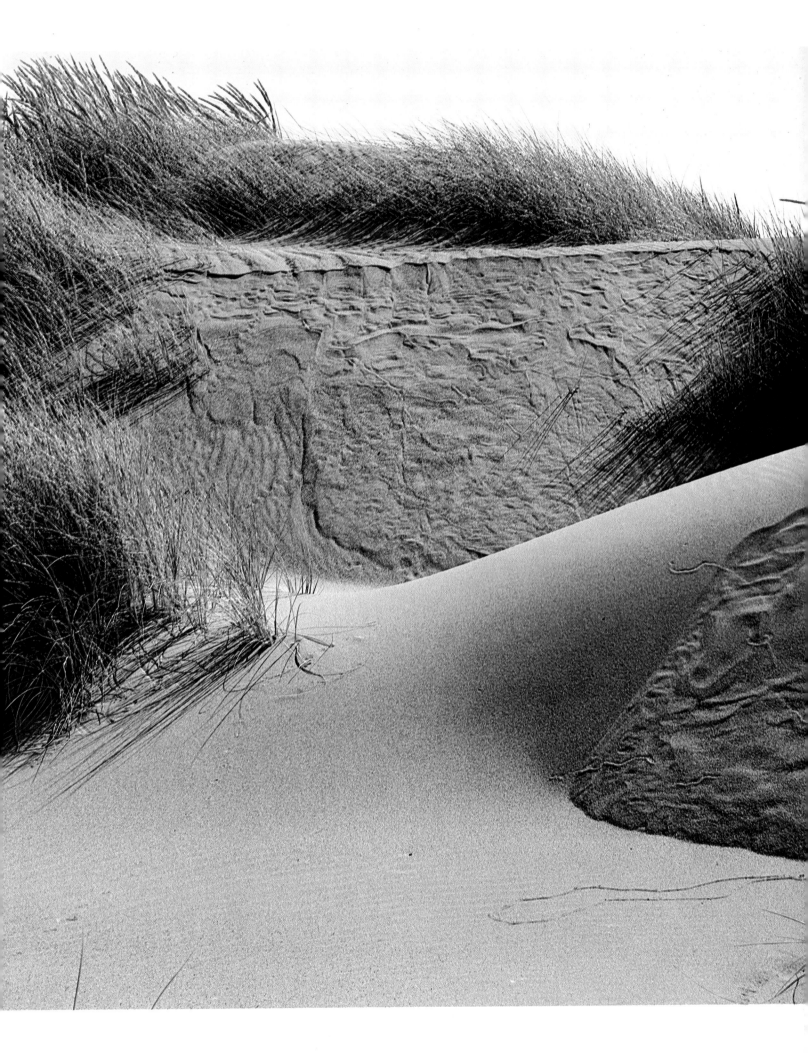

Poppies, Big Sur. The California state flower was first named *Copa de Oro*—cup of gold—by early Spaniards.

Wildflowers and sagebrush, Pt. Lobos.

(left) Throughout southern California, as here in the Holmes Mountains of San Diego, the dominant form of vegetation is chaparral. An association of hardy, dwarfed and drought-resistant shrubs—manzanita, chamise, rhus, ceanothus and scrub oak.

Grasses, lava outcroppings, south of Humbug Mountain, Oregon. More golden even than the hills of California are the grassy coastal swales and meadows of southern Oregon, south from Port Orford to Brookings.

Bigleaf maple above Mill Creek, Redwood National Park.

Chapter 9

Up from Disney Sea

Not far from my home, a five-mile stretch of undeveloped shore gives a stunning glimpse into the passing grandeur of the Pacific. It is, naturally enough, under study for another high-rise development, proposed for the apparent noneconomic reason of adding counterpoint to the vertical thrust of the coastal hills.

Such reasoning stems from what I call the Disney Imperative, the compulsion to create artificial environments out of natural ones. In the rhetoric of the Disney Imperative, unspoiled landscape or seascape is only raw material for "creativity," and technology is the magic wand that will transform it. Sewer outfalls will lead to marine enrichment, oil drill platforms will usher in mariculture, and dredges are to be envisioned as the plowshares of a fertile sea. Although the Pacific shore, with its magnificent redwood forests, rocky headlands, and fertile estuaries, might appear capable of discouraging the Disney Imperative, the Nature Improvers are capable of finding deficiencies in its natural appearance and productivity. Often, of course, these deficiencies are as much in the special perspective of the Nature Improvers as in the shore itself.

Thus, the proponent of counterpointing vertical thrust turns out to be the owner of the coastal property. The endless plains of the ocean similarly cry out for vertical counterpoint, according to the U. S. Geological Survey and others who favor off-shore oil development. Spills from the oil platforms can also relieve the depressing color monotony of the ocean, although their proponents say little about this.

Conversely, along the North Pacific coast there are too many verticals, so clear-cutting and fast-tracts are used as a relief from the redwood and cedar that cut off the view.

The urban environment obviously has use for landscaping and architectural creativity—but why the natural marine environment, already marred by excesses of technological ingenuity? One must realize that the Disney Imperative means more than artistic indulgence. Large portions of the coastal ranges, as well as lands seaward of the mean high tide line, are in the public domain. While lumbermen, mine operators and fast-tract developers grumble about allowing such public land to lie "idle," their buzz-saws and bulldozers hardly convey a sense of public responsibility. The promise of an artificial environment, on the other hand, is entirely to benefit the public. The "wild" shore is not being desecrated but decorated.

Disney Sea is already in the making. The Santa Monica shore consists of a long and spacious beach that abuts on metropolitan Los Angeles. Its present use—as a public beach—is natural enough, in fact too natural. One agency noted for its creativity would construct an offshore breakwater for the protection of boats and to become the basis for an offshore, i.e., artificial beach. And the six-mile-long breakwater will be topped by—let's see if you can respond to the Disney Imperative—no, not barnacles but a freeway. Thus is unmasked one notable Nature Improver: the California Division of Highways. Generous shoulders on the proposed Santa Monica Causeway would accommodate marinas, high-rise apartments and other developments eager to leapfrog public beachfronts and acquire a high-revenue foothold on the "idle" nearshore. In keeping with the Disney Imperative, the highway people cheerfully accept the responsibility for superseding natural processes. If converting the nearshore into a lagoon reduces cleansing circulation, why not lay underwater air hoses to keep the water—and perhaps the pollution—circulating? Curiously enough, local officials have resisted the causeway. The highway people have demonstrated that they don't have closed minds. They have offered to move the freeway off the causeway and onto the existing beach. Artificial offshore reefs would be installed to nurture an artificial beach. That the concept is untested suggests how true the planners remain to the Disney Imperative. A Scripps Institution oceanographer, Douglas Inman, suggests two possible shortcomings: the diversion of sand into deep water and the stimulation of potentially destructive waves. However, a project consultant, James Dunham, says the "greatest single problem of the entire project" will be acquiring enough earth fill for the causeway. Mr. Dunham then nominates a coastal hill range as a suitable "borrow pit." And why not, he asks, borrow from the hills in such a manner as to transform them into the site for another freeway and for terraced tracts?

Proponents of the causeway may be in for some serious competition. Some airport planners see the solution to airport noise not in quieter airplanes but in extending runways out to sea. These runways, seductively fringed with marinas and beaches, are packaged as complete environments, ostensibly soundproofed and not in outfall rights of way. Perhaps the Pacific shore itself will become a borrow pit to accommodate this seaward thrust.

Proposals to reclaim the ocean are endless. One planner who spoke on the "Real Estate Potential of Offshore Island Development" had taken his inspiration not from traditional islands but from offshore oil-drill platforms which could double as real estate if mounted on earth fill. Causeways would connect these oil-drill islands to the mainland. Islands surrounded *entirely* by water didn't make sense. To solve parking space problems, why not convert surplus aircraft carriers into waterfront parking garages? The city of Portland, Oregon, has considered such an addition to its waterscape.

Natural islands can also be upgraded, according to the gospel of the Disney Imperative. The owner of pastoral Santa Cruz Island, off southern California (under consideration for national park status) plans to dredge out part of the scenic shore to accommodate a marina. He doesn't call it a marina, but an "artificial fjord." Part of the shore already boasts a vacation camp in simulated Polynesian style. Progressive developers in Tahiti may see the light and erect igloo hotels.

Estuaries cry out for the exercise of the Disney Imperative. Lacking the grandeur of the rocky shore or the glamour of sandy beaches, the estuaries with their mudflats are in urgent need of improvement. When the environs of a bay near your home are suddenly referred to as "stinking mudflats," you can sniff a developer seeking a tidelands grant. When the stinking mudflats become a "birdbath," it may be inferred that a public agency has found the estuary's natural life support system of little concern. When the birdbath becomes a "game preserve for mosquitoes," the "mud-mills" or dredges are already in place.

As the life-giving qualities of the estuarine zone are gradually destroyed, public agencies become more interested in their survival. However, devotees of the Disney Imperative can capitalize on this: box-office aquariums, where sea lions balance rubber balls on their noses and bark for anchovies. However, this ersatz life support system is not always considered adequate. A new thrust in estuarine improvement emerges. The developer with hopes of relieving coastal monotony with high-rise towers proposed to compress one of southern California's few remaining estuarine areas, Upper Newport Bay, into a luxury residential boat canal. This compression, according to the developer, would actually enhance the area, producing "forests of kelp" and dense marine life. Seaside gardens to rival those of Versailles would seem to be in the making.

The rundown urban waterfront is certainly in need of biological restoration. However, this particular blue thumb was bearing down on a natural estuary. How would the developer's blue thumb outdo existing shellfish beds, finfish communities, waterfowl rafts, and marsh grass islands?

According to a report sponsored by the developer, the promised marine life was to consist in great part of the barnacles and mussels that would colonize the bulkheads. In other words, the "limited" natural productivity of the estuary would be replaced by what sailors call fouling. Waterfowl and shorebirds whose beaks do not equip them to forage along shores of vertical concrete would be replaced by gulls, which can thrive on harbor waste. To improve on marsh grass, the report proposed colonizing the boat canal with eelgrass. Unfortunately, the depth of the proposed canal would limit its ability to reproduce. The public authorities charged with maintaining this marine garden could thus expect to be forever replanting eelgrass. There was still the promise of forests of kelp . . . and also the question of how pleasure-boat propellers were to escape becoming entangled in those forests. The species of kelp involved turned out to be a small one, palm kelp, rather than the giant offshore variety. It, too, would require continual replanting. In fact, the test plants that were installed died within three months. It is doubtful that even an army of scuba divers could keep this garden mirage alive.

Indian middens and fossil deposits around Upper Newport Bay are of great interest to archeologists and paleontologists. When a number of scientists and citizens complained that these rich deposits were being torn up by the bulldozers of one bayside developer, he replied that he looked forward to having his bulldozers "open up" more fossil and Indian deposits.

The Nature Improvers find the chaparral foot-

hills along the coast just as attractive. To begin with, chaparral doesn't look the way a forest should look. Rather than being tall and open, it is short and tangled. It doesn't even grow into timber. Sometimes it exudes a resinous odor that overpowers the aroma of sage and leads one to ask where the oil spill is. To top it off, this nonforest has a tendency to *burn*—the unpardonable sin, particularly when a developer has put a hundred-acre housing tract in the middle of it. And as for the rivers! One drives across bridge after bridge that promises a river—the Santa Ana, the Santa Clara, the Santa Ynez—but one looks in vain for a sign of running water. To navigate these rivers one needs a dune buggy. One wonders why the sign doesn't read "Santa Ana Sands" or "Santa Clara Sands." When winter rains bring water, there is usually too much of it, at least for developers who build in flood plains. A river that reclaims its natural bed cannot be forgiven, and these wild, unruly, unpredictable rivers become known as flood agents.

To the Nature Improvers, the shortcomings of the chaparral watershed have become standing insults. Such unruly rivers and ugly forests prove that nature cannot be left alone. Chaparral is replaced with housing tracts, grazing pastures and *real* trees, i.e., the kind that grow into lumber or give shade. The nonrivers are compressed into concrete flood control channels so that the liberated flood plains can remain forever safe for trailer parks and other cultural artifacts. One cannot pause until the last piece of chaparral has given way to ice plant, the last hillside to terraced developments, and the last streambed to cement. Only then can southern California be free from the scourge of chaparral and seasonal rivers.

The existence of such natural insults is galling enough to the Nature Improvers; that some people would preserve these insults is an exasperation. These people, better known as wilderness freaks, would restrict man's ingenuity by putting limits on development in flood plains and chaparral hillsides. Ironically, this concern can stem less from affection for chaparral watersheds than from the shortcomings of Nature Improvement.

The more development intrudes into the chaparral watersheds, the greater the number of fires that seem to occur, simply because risk and exposure are greater. Hillside houses that don't burn may simply slide away because the natural soil cover, and the stability that goes with it, have been tampered with. Houses that escape burning and sliding may still be exposed to mud slides, once the ugly chaparral that once held the hillsides together no longer exists. Constant irrigation for ornamental plants can undermine artificial slopes. Houses that escape burning, sliding, and mud may still be flooded out. And flood control programs are so costly (up to $2 million a mile) that they invariably run behind flood plain development. Even so, the extent of flood control work is usually such as to retard the natural transport of sand that helps nourish beachfront. Thus coastal communities whose beachfront has already been eroded by upcoast breakwaters find themselves nudged closer to the Pacific. The ugly chaparral and the fickle rivers can achieve what the Nature Improvers never could. Left intact, they serve to maintain the integrity of beaches and hillsides without bankrupting the public treasury for disaster funds and stabilization programs. Chaparral doesn't even require irrigation, much less landscape architects.

Undaunted, disciples of the Disney Imperative now prepare to upgrade the Pacific. Environmental (formerly sanitary) engineers have, by constructive thinking, converted "primary treated"—coarsely-screened—sewage into "organic enrichment." Outfalls thus "fertilize" the ocean; nature's upwelling is not sufficient. Such residual waste nutrients as nitrogen and phosphorus do indeed fertilize estuarine waters, so much so that the surface blooms of algal scum exceed the assimilative capacity of the estuary and accumulate as black, pungent bottom sludge that drives out clean-water, clean-sand, clean-silt animals and plants. As a result, estuarine outfalls are being replaced by outfalls into the open ocean—the answer to pollution being more dilution, as the environmental engineers would have it. Here, however, another curious aspect of fertilization emerges. In recent times, a number of kelp forests in southern California have receded drastically. Many of these ghost forests

exist near outfalls that are supposed to be enriching them. Why such reverse fertilization is occurring is not entirely clear. Dense concentrations of sea urchins occur in these ghost forests. The urchins, which graze on kelp, normally move on to browner pastures, allowing kelp to generate. Scientific investigations now suggest that sewage matter may nourish the urchins. In becoming stationary feeders, urchins may have prevented the kelp from regenerating. In time, the comeback of the urchin-eating sea otter may be of some help in controlling this population explosion. Some scientists suggest that the growth of kelp may also be inhibited because the turbidity produced by sewage particles has reduced the amount of light.

As the case for sewage as a fertilizer is refuted, we hear a new one—for the thermal effluent from coastal power plants. Near one point of thermal discharge in the area of Long Beach, California, one marine species has indeed increased. That species, unfortunately, happens to be the sting ray —and it has to be periodically removed to protect swimmers and lifeguards. The Nature Improvers are now trying to figure out how to discourage this less-than-endearing form of marine life.

More advanced schemes for upgrading the Pacific Ocean are mainly centered around the Santa Barbara Channel. In 1971, Santa Barbara residents read how a new "enhancement to the environment" would provide navigation aids, a small craft haven, a sport fish habitat, and night lighting to augment starlight and moonlight. What might this enhancement be? An environmental impact statement by the U. S. Geological Survey gave the answer: more oil wells in the channel. "How can more obstacles aid navigation?" wondered Lois Sidenberg of Get Oil Out, a citizens' organization. Small boats can't easily be tied up to a platform. Because of its open structure the platform offers no protective lee. The Coast Guard in fact warns boaters to avoid the very structures the Geological Survey would promote as havens for small craft. The notion that marine life can find shelter around oil platforms has led to promoting them as sport fish habitats. The possibility of massive blowouts might appear to discourage this; however, the presence of some marine life around natural oil seeps in the channel has led to the cheerful conclusion that marine life can adapt nicely to artificial oil seeps, including blowouts. Indeed, oil company officials eagerly rummage through Spanish archives for quotations to prove the regular occurrence of natural oil seeps. Unfortunately, recent studies by marine biologist Nancy Nicholson of the University of Southern California indicate that relatively *few* species live within seep areas, natural or otherwise. The settlement of larval barnacles can be temporarily inhibited by oiling the substrate. As a result of such revelations, the natural oil seeps that were supposed to prepare the channel for artificial oil seeps are now depicted as an environmental scourge that must be removed—yes, you guessed it—by extracting the oil. "A vigorous program of carefully controlled drilling and production would eventually eliminate this environmental threat for all time," wrote J. H. Birman, a geologist at Occidental College, in a letter to the *Los Angeles Times.*

In a letter to the same newspaper, Dr. Norman Sanders of the University of California at Santa Barbara pointed out the deficiencies of the "pump it all out" theory. Primary oil recovery methods remove only 30 to 40 percent of the oil present. Pumping out even this modest amount from the shallow channel reservoirs could reduce underground pressures and cause subsidence and settling. (Oil extraction in Long Beach, California, caused one power plant to sink twenty-four feet and to move seven feet sideways.) According to Sanders, fluid injection to deter such subsidence and expedite the recovery of oil could "be dangerous because of the difficulty of precisely controlling injection pressures. Too much pressure would force oil upward, ultimately leaking into the channel." He concluded: "The indisputable fact that oil is still there after millions of years of seismic activity shows that leakage to the surface must be slight. When a major earthquake next strikes the Santa Barbara Channel, the natural seepage would be negligible compared to the amount of oil gushing forth from broken lines, sheared wells, and collapsed storage tanks on shore."

Whatever their seductions, not everything has yielded to the siren songs of the Disney Imperative. No aircraft carrier turned parking lot is anchored off the riverfront in Portland, Oregon. No supercauseway severs Santa Monica from the Pacific Ocean. There is no fjord on Santa Cruz Island. The developer who offered to relieve the monotony of coastal topography with high-rise towers has backed off for the time being.

The same public that became restive about the excesses of the Big Bonanza psychology has been able, when adequately informed, to see through the cosmetic lures of the Disney Imperative. Citizen groups have unmasked the swindle of Nature Improvement. At one time, the fate of Upper Newport Bay seemed virtually sealed. Public officials, impressed by the schemes for transforming a "game preserve for mosquitoes," had entered into a land trade that would have given away public ownership of the shorefront to a private developer. Local citizens led by Mr. and Mrs. Frank Robinson and conservationists well acquainted with the public as well as the natural values of the bay were able to prevent the action. It was not a simple matter of showing people the bay in order to win them over. That was part of the problem. The only public road to the bay was in such disrepair as to be of more benefit to local tow-truck operators. One of the few tangible public improvements was a portable chemical toilet. All but total neglect of the bay was what had doomed it.

As a remedy, the Friends of Newport Bay, chaired by Dr. Charles Greening, decided to sponsor public tours. At first, its publicized reputation discouraged visitors. Who wanted to see mosquitoes? I recall my excitement, just after posting a descriptive brochure on a convenient wooden siding near the bayfront, at having a reader for the brochure materialize before my eyes—a young woman with a baby in her arms. Eagerly, I rushed up to her to elaborate on the value of marsh grass and fiddler crabs. Somewhat anxiously, she assured me of her sympathy. Encouraged, I became loquacious on the intricacies of estuarine food chains. Only afterwards did I realize that my audience had had more pressing matters to attend to. The wooden siding had belonged to that one public improvement, the chemical toilet.

One day Walter Houk, an editor of *Sunset* magazine, made a tour of the bay at the behest of the Friends. He was impressed and published a short article, with photographs showing how the "mud bath" supported birds and fish by the millions. This was enough to attract over six hundred people on a drizzling Saturday morning. Once they had been awakened to the bay's natural vitality and beauty, the public quickly saw through the so-called improvement scheme. Its support for protecting the bay made possible a legal and political campaign that culminated in a court decision finding the land trade unconstitutional that was followed by the election of a new County Board of Supervisors. The suit was brought by Phil Berry of the Sierra Club. The body that had once been persuaded to regard the bay as a worthless mud bath now is working with the state to make it a natural wildlife preserve.

This reversal brought some interesting revelations, economic as well as ecological. In the proposed exchange, the county was to have traded away the public tidelands for three marsh islands owned by the developer. Public tidelands don't come cheap; however, a price tag in the millions of dollars was placed on the marsh islands, so as to make the trade appear to be a fair one. As a part of the agreement, however, the islands newly acquired by the public were to be dredged out to make way for a boat canal, and the dredged spoil was to be used to fill in the tidelands acquired by the developer.

Why, if these islands were worth so much, had the developer been so willing to part with them? Because, as the public authorities now learned, they were subject to flooding and to earthquakes from an active fault less than two miles away. The public will indeed be acquiring these disaster-prone islands—not for removal as fill, but as an integral part of the wildlife preserve and at a price below the previous valuation. From the developer's figure of $10 million, their value has been reappraised by the Interior Department at $189,000.

Today, my son and his classmates visit the bay as part of their nature education. Another frequent visitor is Dr. Joel Hedgpeth, who once felt compelled to classify all estuaries as "shrinking," and whose great-grandfather was one of the first to alienate public tidelands in Oregon. He has been retained as a consultant by the Friends of the Bay. To enlarge on its natural productivity, Dr. Hedgpeth has recommended removing silt (accumulated in the operation of an old salt works) from the upper end of the bay and restoring the bay's tidal prism—a proposal not without irony, as he himself happily concedes, since it means that the bay will indeed see some dredging. But it will not be to remove the marsh islands or turn the bay into a luxury boat canal.

As the shortsightedness of the Disney Imperative becomes more evident, the benefits of conserving and restoring beaches, estuaries, and rocky shore also become more evident. Recently, the number and diversity of fish in San Diego Bay dramatically increased. Were sewage outfalls and thermal discharges responsible? Quite the contrary: the outfalls had been either removed or curtailed. As the bay waters recovered their oxygen balance, sulfurous layers of bottom sludge decomposed, permitting bottom life to revive. The fishermen who once wrote off San Diego Bay now return to share in this renaissance of marine life.

Regulatory agencies are now enacting standards that would seek to prevent degradation in the first place. In California, polluters who had depended on the ocean as a "free" sewage sink have discovered that it can be cheaper to treat and reuse their streams of waste. Sewage recycling may not appear as glamorous as the conceits of the Disney Imperative, but it promises to be far more effective in protecting the Pacific shore.

The willingness of so many people to change their attitudes even extends to the way they govern themselves. There are almost as many political jurisdictions involved in coastal affairs as there are species of fish—a regulatory overkill that tends to limit perspectives. City and county boundaries arbitrarily cut up the shore piecemeal, ignoring wide-ranging marine processes such as sand transport, nutrient flow, and salmon migrations. This piecemeal regulation has tended to complicate rather than resolve coastal problems, and is frustrating to citizens. However counterproductive, the practice has been enshrined in political folklore as "home rule"—a concept that has too often been a pushover for the Nature Improvers. Citizens and conservationists have joined with political theorists in urging that the coastal zone be treated as a regional resource rather than a piecemeal commodity. After legislation for this purpose was repeatedly bottled up in the California legislature, the California Coastal Alliance gathered 300,000 signatures in order to place the legislation on a statewide ballot.

Opponents of the bill were quick to react. Standard Oil of California donated $30,000 to defeat the measure. Southern Pacific Land Company came forth with $20,000. The Irvine Company—the advocate of converting Upper Newport Bay into a boat canal—chipped in $50,000. Whittaker and Baxter, a firm with a long record of defeating such measures on behalf of well-heeled clients, was retained to "handle" the Coastal Initiative. A "Citizens' Corporation" raised a $1.1 million "public education" fund.

Billboards went up proclaiming, "Conservation Yes, Confiscation No." Four-color brochures asked ominously, "Who is trying to do what to California?" Broadsides, billboards, and five-figure campaign donations notwithstanding, the voters of California approved a California State Coastal Zone Conservation Commission by a 55 percent majority, authorized to develop a coastal plan in three years, and with interim control over development. Its charter is to "preserve, protect, and where possible, to restore the resources of the coastal zone . . . a distinct and valuable resource belonging to all the people." Trailer parks and motels have been denied permits to develop prime agricultural lands. Thus the artichoke and broccoli fields of central California may still have a chance. Proposed marinas that would unhinge the shoreline and fill in the estuaries have been rebuffed even more firmly. A permit to build a 639-unit coastal condominium complex was recently denied. Noting that 244 persons over the age of 62 would be displaced by this improvement, the Commission staff declared, "The issue is whether the elderly, many of whom are long-time residents of the area, should be deprived of the opportunity to live in the coastal zone by the actions of the private housing market and of public agencies." One high-rise condominium now advertises itself as "the last of the big time splendors."

Such policies have helped to cool the land speculation that fueled premature subdivision and that hounded Jeffers at Carmel. The pressure to urbanize agricultural land is often increased by assessing agricultural land at its "highest and best" rather than its current use. Use-related assessment might serve to prevent coastal agriculture from becoming obsolete.

The Commission has not been without criticism; original supporters have expressed concern that the Commission has granted too many development permits prior to implementing strong planning criteria and thus has lost important planning options. At the same time, some state legislators have attempted to condition approval of Commission planning funds on greater regulatory leniency.

In both structure and purpose, the California Coastal Zone Commission is a notable departure from politics as usual, an indication that the people of the Pacific shore have recognized the value of the unique resource that is theirs. Whether such political developments can make the change in attitude a lasting rather than a momentary trend remains to be seen. As we shall see, the physical nature of the Pacific shore has its own dramatic way of emphasizing the need for such change.

Chapter 10

Strategic Retreat from the Shore

You can see the shorefront of Crescent City in northern California without having to go and stand on it. No chain stores, power plants, elevated freeways, or glassy condominiums shut off the view. The beach that slopes gently towards the tide is sand, not concrete, and at its back are vistas of green park land, not a commercial strip.

It would be pleasant to think that community appreciation of the esthetic values of the shore had been responsible for the situation, but this is not entirely so. Crescent City's spacious shorefront is the belated result of having recognized another underrated virtue of the Pacific shore: its value for storm protection.

Seismic sea waves and the earthquakes that cause them are as natural to the region as ocean sunsets and abalone. Earthquakes inland are terrifying enough, but a coastal earthquake has an extra dimension of disaster. The motion that can lift up the land or dash it downwards can haul buildings and entire city blocks into the Pacific Ocean, exactly as Jeffers predicted: "Some day this coast will dip and be clean." Dredged-out harbor basins have been left high and dry. A difference in elevation of only three or four feet can mean either safety or devastation. Settling and subsidence after an earthquake can bring about this deadly difference. You can be in a housing tract a hundred feet above sea level and still find yourself inundated. A house site on an ocean bluff may be susceptible

to possible slides with or without earthquake nudges. People in search of "white-water" views take just that risk every day.

Although the effects of an earthquake itself are localized, seismic sea waves triggered by a local quake can wash ashore thousands of miles away. The relative infrequency of earthquakes and seismic sea waves is in fact one reason they can be so deadly. On the Gulf and Atlantic coasts, hurricanes occur with a frequency that calls for vigilant attention to safeguards against possible damage. Major earthquakes may occur at intervals of thirty or forty years, so that despite all the dramatic literature on the phenomenon, their likelihood may still seem remote. The metropolitan area around San Francisco Bay is built along the San Andreas fault, where earthquakes have occurred repeatedly, and where the intense concentration of urban activity is nothing less than a disaster waiting to happen. The consequences of an earthquake depend less on the force of the quake than on natural and social conditions seemingly quite independent of it. An assessment of potential damage must take into account such phenomena as the stage of the tide, the structure of the soil, the time of year, even the time of day. To be made homeless by a tidal wave in midsummer and in stormy midwinter are very different matters and likewise with whether it occurs at noon or at midnight.

The 1964 earthquake in Alaska tilted the ocean

bottom, triggering seismic sea waves that traveled down the eastern Pacific coast. The damage was confined to a relatively few harbor areas, and the amount of damage in each generally amounted to less than a quarter of a million dollars—with one notable exception. Crescent City, with a population of 2600, suffered over $10 million in property damage. Eleven lives were lost. What made the difference here?

A seismic wave in the open ocean is only three or four feet high. As it nears the shore, however, such a wave may build up to heights of thirty or sometimes even one hundred feet. The gradient and shape of the seabed may reduce or magnify a seismic sea wave. Thus, certain Pacific basin communities seem especially vulnerable. Hilo, Hawaii, was visited by seismic waves in 1946, 1952, 1957, and 1960. Coastal geography was what worked against Crescent City. Although in other communities in Oregon and California the runup was slight, in Crescent City the water at high tide rose twenty-one feet above mean low-low water. A series of seismic waves struck around high tide, and thus the runup was maximized. Entire city blocks lay under six feet of water, and the runup extended over a mile inland. While many coastal communities are set on the bluffs that are typical of the Pacific shore, Crescent City occupies a low-lying plain. In its rapid rise and exit, this mass of water pummeled at buildings with terrible force. Much of the damage, however, came as a result of the lumber industry, a major local activity. Stumps, slash, and other debris litter the shore, providing material for children to build forts and for artists to concoct driftwood montages on a grand scale. This debris, lifted on the shoulders of a seismic sea wave, literally rose up against the town, pounding it into splinters.

Crescent City also serves as an oil storage area. As elsewhere, the tanks for this purpose are built close to the shore, exposing them to coastal storm damage. Basil Wilson and Alf Torun wrote in *The Tsunami of the 1964 Alaskan Earthquake,* "Invariably oil spillage caused by an earthquake or its tsunami results in fire, which can spread rapidly and make a holocaust of any coastal town or city." One of the waves that hit Crescent City hurled a gasoline truck into an electrical junction box. The resulting fire spread to a tank farm, where it burned for three days.

But all this structural damage, though severe, was not what caused the loss of life. After four seismic sea waves had risen and receded, people returned downtown to assess the damage. It was then that the fifth and largest seismic sea wave struck, and that the eleven people drowned. There is no way of knowing which in a train of seismic waves will be the last, or the worst. Crescent City, in thoughtless partnership with the seismic forces of the Pacific basin, had invited a disaster to happen —without being ready when the invitation was finally accepted.

Coastal disaster can be invited in other ways. The mud deposits of which estuarine tidelands often consist make a weak building foundation. Fill can overload the loose deposits, causing mud to ooze out along the edge of a fill. A geologist, Harold Goldman, reported in the San Francisco Bay Plan Supplement: "Past earthquakes show that such poor ground is a greater potential hazard than is nearness to the fault or the center of the earthquake. For example, in the 1906 San Francisco earthquake, shaking was much more violent in the waterfront areas underlain by bay mud and fill than Nob Hill and similar areas with more solid rock at or near the surface."

Water-saturated soils can even liquefy and flow, so that residents who had thought of themselves as comfortably above the Pacific are transported directly into the tides. Inland, the risk of liquefaction and settling is one thing; next to an ocean, with its prospect of flooding, it is another thing altogether. When an earthquake and waterfront settling are combined with heavy winter rains, two awesome flooding agents are at work in deadly concert. Ruptured sewers and water mains add to the deluge not only volume, but the threat of typhoid and hepatitis as well.

Some reclaimed tidelands are not filled and elevated above the high tide line since it may be cheaper just to build a perimeter tidal dike, as is done in Holland. Here settling or sliding is not a necessary prerequisite for flooding; just one fracture in the dike—or its foundation—is sufficient. In a coastal earthquake, such a break in the dike can be as easy as snapping a twig. A subaqueous slide can set up local wave action and, if it is on a large enough scale, seismic sea waves as well. Deep dredging of ship channels to accommodate supertankers can increase this hazard. *The Safety of Fills,* a report made for the San Francisco Bay Conservation and Development Commission, contains this observation:

> Present plans call for deepening the main shipping channels in the Bay from 35 to 45 feet. Unless proper measures are taken, the potential for subaqueous slides under dynamic loading may increase as the channels are deepened, and concomitantly there could be an increase in the potential for serious hazard to some Bayside locations either directly from slides and/or possibly from slide induced waves. Also, subaqueous slides could cause serious damage to utility and communication lines.

Another source of added risk is the unhinging of natural storm protection features, such as dune fields and beaches, in the interests of shore improvement. Millions of dollars' worth of shore protection, built without the aid of a single government contract, can be obliterated in a project designed to bring development a few steps closer to the water. High winter tides and coastal storm waves are often sufficient to create havoc here; the introduction of a coastal earthquake or a seismic wave turns into catastrophe.

There are still other ways of inviting the ocean to take over. In the modest town of Aliso, at the southern tip of San Francisco Bay, even though there has been no shorefront development to cut off the view, you still need a ladder to see the bay. The obstruction, a huge tidal dike resembling a World War I bunker, had to be erected because Aliso was gradually sinking below the bay water level. A reduction in underground water pressure, brought on by farmers who were depleting groundwater sources to irrigate fruit orchards, had caused the town to settle and sink. Although tidal dikes can help keep out the Pacific—at least in intervals between strong seismic jolts—they can also serve

to impound the runoff from winter rains. To escape ponding, many houses in Aliso are perched on stiltlike brick and earthfill foundations. Bayfront houses and firms in need of similar uplift often put up roadside signs reading "Clean Fill Wanted." In the sinking town of Aliso, where people cannot afford to be so choosy, hand-lettered signs read simply "Fill Wanted."

Over a period of thirty years, parts of Long Beach, California, have sunk twenty-four feet as a result of underground oil extraction. Subsidence served to rupture pipelines, oil well casings, utility lines, and building foundations, as land that had once been ten feet above sea level sank to ten feet below. The cost of remedial work, including massive tidal dikes, exceeded $100 million. The subsidence of the coast haunted the defense industry in World War II, since the affected area included the sprawling Long Beach naval shipyards. Construction crews found themselves simultaneously fighting a war and underground subversion.

The Chumash Indians of Santa Rosa Island, urged on by Franciscan missionaries, forsook their island culture for the mainland mission system to escape the force of coastal storms. Crescent City found that safety could be bought at a lesser price. Over the years, sand had accumulated along the harborfront road, widening the shore by over seven hundred feet—an addition that belonged to the city. The city fathers began to see a real estate paradise in the making, with luxury hotels and restaurants hawking elegant access to the shore and recharging the municipal treasury. Some residents resisted commercializing the public shore, but many others supported it.

If the seismic waves had visited Crescent City three or four years later, after the plans for development had become a reality, the toll of lives lost and of property damaged might easily have been doubled. As things were, an "undeveloped" shoreline helped buffer Crescent City against the full brunt of waves twenty feet high. Today all the real estate schemes have been scrapped. The windfall beach strip is now designated a safety zone devoted mainly to public recreation. Crescent City may never hit the big time as cities go. But one can still walk along its open waterfront and enjoy the priceless qualities that enthralled J. Ross Browne a century ago—the soaring sea gulls, the rebound of the surf, the vast sea "stretching so far away from the petty vexations of life, that there is nothing left in me of envy, jealousy, malice, or hatred; nothing but love for the good, true, and pure."

While Crescent City learned to respect the natural character of the Pacific shore, other communities have persisted in flirting with havoc. Seen from the air, sewage treatment plants, skyscrapers, and parking lots crowd to the edge, as if preparing to charge. Even though the 1906 San Francisco earthquake demonstrated the risks of building on filled land, the biggest boom in landfill was still to come, carrying out a prophecy made in 1907 by the U. S. Geological Survey: "It is very probable that the new San Francisco to rise on the ruins will be to a large extent a *duplicate* of the former city in defects of construction." It was not until the late 1960s, with the creation of the San Francisco Bay Conservation and Development Commission, that regulations began to be imposed on the booming land-fillers. As these measures were being put into belated effect, a conference was held in San Francisco on geological hazards in the western United States. Speaker after speaker emphasized how geological features—landslides, faults, soil strength—should be considered by public officials in charge of planning coastal development. Jack Schoop, who was then chief planner for the San Francisco Bay Conservation and Development Commission, recalled his experiences in a coastal city shaken by the Good Friday earthquake of 1964, while he was planning director for Anchorage, Alaska. During that earthquake, part of Turnagain-by-the-Sea, an exclusive residential section, slipped into Cook Inlet. The houses there had been built on an unstable slope and the earthquake triggered a landslide. Schoop told of the measures taken to avoid future disasters:

A task force labeled the most hazardous areas around the downtown, all the areas overlooking Cook Inlet and Ship Creek, around which Anchorage is built . . . They were labeled areas in which either nothing should be built or whatever is built should be light and able to take future slide activities . . . But somewhere, and I reckon it about the 45th day after Good Friday, a louder noise was heard. It was the scramble of disaster-affected owners—which was almost everyone, it seemed—to get their projects going, to get in *first* . . . It became a really heady pell-mell, and the last ones to be listened to as that crescendo mounted now were the planners and geologists.

The task force maps that federal forces, as well as local ones, had prepared, indicating hazard areas and what ought to be avoided, were ignored. A future governor of Alaska was to show how you go in and rebuild by building a very, very flashy new hotel—a high-rise hotel—right in one of those hazard areas. Areas which should have been left open, or at least held down to single-family density, according to the task force maps, were being rebuilt with apartment houses. The political pressure mounted on even the federal task force—which was not immune—to water down the warnings in these task force ratings of the hazard area. Even though they were being ignored, they still were an obstacle to getting in there. And they were, in fact, watered down—*twice* . . . Two years after the earthquake—two years—the remnants of those who cared about the future of Anchorage met at my house; we concluded that this tide was so strong it could not be reversed. It was going to have to run its course. That's when I finally did "get out of the way."

Whether the attitude of Crescent City, which tried to come to terms with its natural environment, or of Anchorage, which continues to defy it and to court the prophecy of Robinson Jeffers, will be the one that prevails in the future, no one can be sure. What one can be sure of is that the natural forces of the Pacific shore will continue to assert themselves, and that other coastal communities will sooner or later be presented with a similar choice.

Chapter 11

The Century-Old Laugh

A utility executive recently complained that pending legislation might delay the construction of a coastal power plant. "You talk about how long it takes to build a power plant; apparently you haven't thought about how long it takes to build a coastline," replied Alan Sieroty, a California legislator and a principal architect of the California Coastal Zone Conservation Commission.

It has taken a while, but the philosophical heirs of Muir and Jeffers are finally being elected to public office. The Pacific shore is by no means unique in inspiring ardent defenders and admirers, particularly in this new age of environmental awareness. Yet because of its vulnerable character, the sheer industrial energy aimed at it, and the Faustian predicament that has been the result, the consciences of artists, scientists, and citizens have been goaded with a special intensity.

Robinson Jeffers was pessimistic about the ability of "social up-lifters" to counter what he saw as the "meanness" of industrial civilization. If his pessimism had prevailed, motorways would bisect Olympic National Park and the Oregon shore would be off limits to nonproperty owners. Behind every coastal park, every free-flowing river, and every restored seal rookery, has stood a dedicated band of citizens and enlightened public officials prepared to buck the conventional wisdom.

After so many years of contention over offshore oil development, California has finally taken a modest but significant step to reduce energy demands: mandatory standards for housing insulation so we don't live in thermal sieves. Housing insulation, sewage reclamation, smaller watercloset, and paper recycling may not seem as glamorous as keeping oil wells out of the Santa Barbara Channel or keeping mudflats in Upper Newport Bay, but they are just as essential to a more stable existence. To conserve resources and liberate its coast from litter, Oregon restricts use of throwaway containers. This willingness to modify our demands on coastal resources must transcend the urge to simply shift exploitive pressures to somebody else's coastal zone. Such emergent reforms tend to counter the cultural cliché that Americans prefer technical "fixes" to changes in social convenience.

In the future, as we take our grandchildren to the shore to build sand castles, find surfing waves or catch silver salmon, we may find out whether or not the Yurok Indians had good reason to laugh. With evergreen forests on one side, bronze sea forests on the other and the shore between, the coastal Indians developed enough cultural wisdom to live, laugh, and endure for over three thousand years—an accomplishment we are beginning to recognize as far more commendable than any exploit we can claim as our own.

Pacific Coast Gazetteer

California

Cabrillo National Monument, at the tip of the Point Loma peninsula near San Diego, provides a magnificent overview of the Pacific shore. The monument is easily reached from downtown San Diego over a scenic, sign-posted route. There are exhibits of the Spanish period and commercial whaling days, and a historic lighthouse that is one of the better vantage points for a view of migrating gray whales. The migration to lagoon calving grounds off Baja California begins in late November and continues into February, peaking around mid-January. On weekends during the migration season, rangers lecture on whale behavior. (Other headlands for whale spotting include Laguna Beach in Orange County, the Palos Verdes Peninsula at Los Angeles, and Point Dume, in the Malibu region north of Los Angeles. Whale-watching boats operate out of San Diego, San Clemente, Newport Beach and Los Angeles.)

The view from the monument extends south into Baja California, and includes the Coronados Islands. The outer edge of San Diego Bay is clearly visible as a long sand spit (often referred to as Silver Strand), where there are naval facilities, a resort and popular public beaches. The spit would not exist today, however, except for extensive sand hauls that have served to stem erosion since 1940. The spit's natural source of sand is the Tijuana River watershed to the south, and a dam on this watershed built by the Mexican government has cut into the sand supply.

The peninsular community of Coronado contains the Hotel Coronado, a charming architectural landmark from the Victorian era. Directly to the south are modern condominium towers whose adverse effect on physical and visual access to the shore has led to sharp restrictions on the construction of high-rise buildings.

Farther south, the circular outline of a modern concrete bullring marks the Mexican border. An open beach and salt marsh lie on the U. S. side. A surplus naval facility here could have become the site of a nuclear power plant, a refinery or a dredged harbor. Instead, however, the federal government released the 372 acres to California with the stipulation that it was to become a state park. Border Field State Park has a minimum of public facilities and is relatively uncongested, with plenty of room for hikers and migratory birds. Threats to natural features include possible channelization and filling of the marsh estuary outside the park's boundaries.

Extensive recreational activities may be observed in the bay itself. Its waters, once under swimming quarantine as a result of sewage discharges, have been upgraded thanks to aggressive action by the California Regional Water Quality Board in San Diego. The Board has also begun working with

Mexican authorities to see that sewage discharges south of the border do not contaminate San Diego beaches, as occurred in the 1950s and 1960s.

From the monument one may also observe the lush brown canopy of a kelp forest that rims Point Loma's seaward side. This submarine forest shelters lobsters, abalone and schools of small fish. It receded drastically in the 1950s and early 1960s. An explosion in the population of kelp-grazing sea urchins was a major reason for this recession. The urchins were eventually controlled by quicklime, permitting the kelp to revive. Today one may see boats harvesting the kelp for chemical and industrial uses. (Other restoration projects were under way in 1974 off the Palos Verdes peninsula at Los Angeles.)

San Diego's MISSION BAY AQUATIC PARK, reclaimed from an ecologically important mudflat (especially vital to migratory birds), swarms with plush hotels, restaurants and bayside parking lots. Although this park is a considerable advance over the usual cluttered urban waterfront, the ocean's natural productivity has been severely altered by wholesale dredge and fill operations. Only a pathetic, hard-to-find, postage-stamp-sized marsh "refuge" on the north side of the park has been spared. Such token preservation is obviously not the way to ensure a living flyway along the southern Pacific shore. More comprehensive proposals for refuges in TIJUANA SLOUGH at the border, UPPER NEWPORT BAY at Newport Beach, and MORRO BAY were pending in 1974. One was established at SEAL BEACH NAVAL WEAPONS STATION south of Long Beach.

SEA WORLD, a commercial aquarium located in the park, contains a live tidepool exhibit where children may handle starfish. One may also watch seals balance balls on their noses. (I wonder whether seals would be civilized enough to enjoy watching human beings balance balls on *their* noses.)

At Scripps Institution of Oceanography at nearby La Jolla, the VAUGHAN AQUARIUM-MUSEUM has live exhibits of California marine life in re-created tidepool, kelp, nearshore and wharf piling habitats—everything from sharks to moray eels. Models depict physical processes such as beach formation and deep-sea oceanographic investigations. The museum bookstore contains a wide selection of marine-oriented books, including natural history guides. Immediately north of the Scripps pier is a marine life preserve where anyone is welcome to look at tidal life (but not to collect it). (Similar rocky shore preserves have been set aside at LAGUNA BEACH, NEWPORT BEACH, and DANA POINT in southern California, and at PACIFIC GROVE in the Monterey area; there are still others along the Oregon coast. Follow La Jolla Shores Boulevard north of La Jolla to reach the museum. The boulevard also happens to contain one of San Diego's first bikeways.)

North of the city of San Diego is TORREY PINES, one of the most scenic of California state parks, a coastal bluff rising sheer from a thin lip of sand. At the top of the bluff, you can feel like a conquistador discovering the Pacific all over again. At the base of the bluff, with the surf roaring in, one feels thousands of miles away from freeways and smog alerts. The park's name refers to a wind-sculptured stand of pines belonging to a species found only here and on SANTA ROSA ISLAND, with the unique ability to sink its roots hundreds of feet into sandstone. A citizens' group, the Torrey Pines Association, has raised funds for expanding the park to include part of LOS PENASQUITOS LAGOON, the haunt of the fiddler crab and ideal habitat for numerous shorebirds.

The community of OCEANSIDE, in northern San Diego County, is a tragic example of beach erosion. A once beautiful beach strand, thronged with surfers and swimmers, is now strewn with cobbles. Upcoast, jetties for a military harbor and a pleasure marina have blocked the natural transport of sand. In neighboring Carlsbad, the BUENA VISTA LAGOON REFUGE off Interstate 5 offers good birding.

The mouth of the SANTA MARGARITA RIVER, visible from the coastal freeway just north of Oceanside, is a nesting ground of the endangered least tern. To protect the birds, the coastal proprietor, the U. S. Marine Corps, suspends training operations during the nesting season. Other nesting grounds include the mouth of SAN DIEGO

CREEK at San Diego, and HUNTINGTON BEACH STATE PARK near the mouth of the SANTA ANA RIVER on the northern boundary of Newport Beach.

The northern end of the CAMP PENDLETON MARINE BASE is occupied by a prominent shore "improvement": the San Onofre nuclear power plant. (As a new game to keep your children occupied on long coastal auto trips, you might see who can count the most power plants.) The new SAN ONOFRE STATE PARK attempts to coexist with this massive industrial intrusion, providing access to scenic coastal sandstone bluffs—which the power plant people would like to "move back" to make way for expansion. Directly north of the power plant and park is President Nixon's Western White House, landscaping and all. At Crescent Bay Point in Laguna Beach, one can observe Seal Rock, one of the last remaining seal-hauling rocks off the southern California mainland.

UPPER NEWPORT BAY at Newport Beach, about an hour's drive south from Los Angeles, provides a glimpse into southern California's fading estuarine scene. Back Bay Road, partially graded and sometimes closed in the rainy winter season, runs along the eastern bayfront. Turn off Coast Highway at Jamboree Road and then turn left onto Back Bay Road just before reaching the Newporter Inn. In winter blue herons, rafts of pintails, avocets and even white pelicans may be spotted. The waters yield spotfin croaker, turbot and littleneck clams. For further information see *Natural Resources of Upper Newport Bay*, issued by the California Fish and Game Department, *I Share This Marsh* by Joan Coverdale, and an excellent history, *Newport Bay* by Ellen Lee (Newport Beach Historical Society, 1974). The Friends of Newport Bay (Box 4088, Irvine, California 92664) schedule guided tours of the bay during winter. The archeology, fossils and geology of the area are analyzed along with ecological aspects. A proposal by the abutting landowner to turn the bay into a predominantly private boat canal was rebuffed. Plans more in tune with the bay's natural character were under consideration in 1974. Newly emplaced barbed wire fences cut across well-beaten paths along the bay's perimeter. A history of public use of the bay has led to a prescriptive easement suit in the courts. On the oceanfront, at DORY FISH MARKET next to the Newport Beach fishing pier, dorymen come ashore daily with fresh-caught fish. Historically, inshore schools of mackerel were seined along this gently sloping beach, horses being used to pull the nets ashore. The pier is located at the head of Newport submarine canyon, which provided relatively calm water for docking ships in bygone coastal trading days. The tip of Newport Beach peninsula gives a view of the harbor jetties that have suppressed the wave action that made the ocean ideally suited to board surfing. It was here that Hawaiian board surfing was introduced to California. Ironically, the upcoast jetty has amplified the waves to produce a prime body surfing area (known as the Wedge). *Only the most advanced body surfers should attempt riding these steep-cresting waves.* Most people just watch.

HUNTINGTON BEACH, just north of Newport Beach, is making an admirable attempt to reclaim its shorefront from the sprawl produced by one of California's first coastal oil bonanzas. The beach is a favorite for pismo clamming. Board surfing may be observed from a pier. To the north of the city, the California Fish and Game Department, with commendable cooperation from Signal Oil Company, plans to restore the BOLSA CHICA MARSHLANDS, which have been altered by oil operations.

CABRILLO BEACH MARINE MUSEUM, 3720 Stephen White Drive, San Pedro, at the extreme end of the Los Angeles harbor, is open to the public free of charge. It can be reached via Pacific Avenue from Harbor Freeway. The museum contains marine fossils, a shell collection, marine life displays, and historical exhibits. Pamphlets giving directions for exploring nearby tidepools are available. The museum director, John Olgium, has been active in protecting tidepools and is also an excellent source of information on the grunion runs that occur at night along southern California beaches in the wake of peak tides. A single female grunion can deposit two thousand eggs in a crib of sand three inches deep within about thirty seconds. One of the few beaches within convenient reach of Los

Angeles inner city residents, Cabrillo Beach is periodically threatened with conversion into a luxury marina.

POINT FERMIN PARK, atop the bluff overlooking Cabrillo Beach, gives an excellent view of the Los Angeles harbor area, smog permitting, and of CATALINA ISLAND across the San Pedro Channel. On the unstable bluffs immediately to the east of the park may be observed the shattered foundations of houses destroyed by landslides. Parks are a safer, much less costly form of land use in such geological situations. In the harbor area itself, a power plant that subsided as a consequence of oil drilling may be observed off Seaside Boulevard in the Desmond bridge area.

In SANTA MONICA, a fishing pier that narrowly escaped demolition in a recent civic controversy is a nostalgic place for strolling. (Note the classic merry-go-round.) Santa Monica has preserved its scenic (and geologically unstable) coastal bluffs as parkland, just as Laguna Beach has done. Santa Monica authorities wanted to limit the height of an apartment building which obstructs the view at the northern end of the blufftop park, but the city of Los Angeles, which had controlling political jurisdiction, overruled the desires of its civic neighbor.

To the north of metropolitan Los Angeles, where Topanga Canyon Road intersects Coast Highway, the SANTA MONICA MOUNTAINS meet the Pacific Ocean in a dramatic shoreline of bluffs and cove beaches. No other urban region contains a largely undeveloped coastal range with twenty-six miles of ocean front. By 1970, pressures were mounting for urbanizing and terracing the range into view lots and fast tracts. Plans for a growth-inducing freeway or coastal causeway had been halted by environmental groups. In 1972 the Ventura–Los Angeles Mountain and Coastal Study Commission, established by the state legislature, recommended an extensive open space plan for the region and a permit system that would closely regulate development in the interim. A Toyon National Urban Park has also been proposed. Unlike the area off Palos Verdes peninsula, this oceanfront is still rimmed by fish-rich kelp forests. Over a hundred

archeological sites have been identified. For further information, see the Commission's *Final Report to the California State Legislature,* available from the California Joint Legislative Committee on Open Space, Sacramento, California 95814.

The SANTA BARBARA MUSEUM OF NATURAL HISTORY, on Mission Canyon Road in Santa Barbara, displays the area's natural and archeological features, including Chumash Indian artifacts. Within walking distance are a handsome botanic garden and the restored SANTA BARBARA MISSION. A classic case of altered beach processes may be observed at the tip of the Santa Barbara harbor breakwater. The breakwater has slowed the nearshore transport of sand, and the sand spit that has formed at the breakwater tip as a result perpetually threatens to encircle the harbor. A dredge must continually suck up the invading sand and pipe it downcoast to beaches threatened with erosion because of the interruption of the natural process. Oil platforms may be viewed offshore—including Platform A, which triggered the infamous 1969 blowout. The Northern CHANNEL ISLANDS, the largest of which is SANTA CRUZ ISLAND, may also be viewed offshore. In 1974 the Los Padres chapter of the Sierra Club was spearheading a drive for a Channel Islands National Park to protect such features as a sea elephant rookery. The University of California at Santa Barbara overlooks GOLETA SLOUGH, which would have been bisected by a freeway except for the opposition of students and faculty, led by the geographer Norman Sanders.

POINT LOBOS RESERVE STATE PARK, five miles south of Carmel on State Highway One, preserves the stunning beauty of the central California coast. Here Edward Weston made his famous still-life photographs of the rocky shore, Robinson Jeffers received the inspiration for his poem "Tamar," and, according to legend, Robert Louis Stevenson was inspired to write *Treasure Island.* For further information on the extensive literary associations with this area, see *The Seacoast of Bohemia* by Franklin Walker (Santa Barbara: Peregrine Smith, 1973). In addition to sea lions, you may spot a sea otter, one of the marine mammals that have come back from near extinction. To sleep in the water, these animals anchor themselves by a strand of kelp. Awake, they may be seen diving for abalone or sea urchins, or using a rock to crack open a meal while floating on their backs. The protection of the reserve extends to subtidal life offshore. Monterey cypresses rim the headlands.

North of Monterey Bay are prime agricultural lands that have been planted to artichokes and broccoli, but which may soon be subdivided into space for motels, trailer parks, and housing tracts. Beautiful cut-flower fields along the northern San Diego County coast are similarly threatened.

South of the reserve, State Highway One skirts the coastal SANTA LUCIA MOUNTAINS, which so intimidated Cabrillo's sailors. This coast contains the southern limit of the redwood country and the well-known BIG SUR AREA.

The SAN FRANCISCO MARITIME STATE HISTORIC PARK, at 2905 Hyde Street in the Fisherman's Wharf section of San Francisco, memorializes the era of coastal trade in exhibits; restored period vessels, including a three-masted sailing ship, are moored at dockside. (Open 10 A.M. to 6 P.M. Monday through Thursday, 10 A.M. to 10 P.M. Friday and Saturday, 10 A.M. to 8 P.M Sunday.) The SAN FRANCISCO MARITIME MUSEUM is located at Polk and Beach Streets. The director, Karl Kortun, is an expert on California maritime history. The LOWIE MUSEUM OF ANTHROPOLOGY at the University of California at Berkeley contains considerable material on California Indians. BANCROFT LIBRARY, on the campus, excels in Western Americana.

STEINHART AQUARIUM, in the Natural History Museum at the center of GOLDEN GATE PARK, exhibits many Pacific fishes in tanks, as well as some marine mammals. The ebb and flow of tides is reproduced in tidepool exhibits. This very popular aquarium can be crowded on the weekends; the prospective visitor is advised to go on a weekday if possible.

The SAN FRANCISCO BAY REGION is fortunate in the number of guides by naturalists, scientists and writers that are available. Many of these can be obtained at the Natural History Museum bookstore. (One of the best is Joel Hedgpeth's *Intro-*

duction to Seashore Life of the San Francisco Bay Region and the Coast of Northern California, published by the University of California Press.) While visiting the aquarium, one should take note of the lush vegetation in Golden Gate Park, which originally consisted of windswept sand dunes. A primary source of irrigation for the trees and flowers (and even the ornamental ponds) is treated sewage, which would normally be shunted by outfall into the bay or ocean. This alternative to ocean dumping is being utilized more and more often, as discharge standards and treatment costs rise. (The San Diego suburb of Santee utilizes its effluent to nourish a chain of public recreation lakes. At the Whittier Narrows water reclamation plant in Los Angeles, depleted groundwater basins are recharged. The Kaiser steel plant in Fontana, California, recycles its effluent, so that there is no need for a waterfront location in order to obtain and dispose of the water it uses.)

The Bay area has been in the forefront of other marine conservation issues. Many freeways that converge upon San Francisco, as a visitor will note, abruptly terminate downtown. Never-opened cloverleaf ramps jut into space. In a pioneering revolt, the city's citizens successfully resisted massive interchanges, doubledeck freeways and other scenic blockbusters. Subsequently, the city helped pass a regional bond issue for the Bay Area Rapid Transit system, called BART.

Although dumps and residential marinas may be observed along the bayfront, such traditional insults to bay ecology are coming to an end. Recognizing that wholesale reclamation could gradually shrink the bay into a polluted navigation channel, the state legislature established the San Francisco Bay Conservation and Development Commission to regulate as well as plan for the bay as a living resource. (*The San Francisco Bay Plan Supplement,* published by the Commission and available from the State Printing Office in Sacramento, provides insight into urban bay problems and serves as a guide to environmental planning.)

In the RICHMOND AREA north of Berkeley one can observe the tremendous appetite of coastal oil refinery and storage operations for real estate. Further north, in the MARTINEZ AREA, the Victorian homestead of John Muir, the pioneer conservationist and founder of the Sierra Club, is now a National Historic Site. Muir never had to contend with the site's new neighbor, a freeway.

In the SOUTH BAY AREA, extensive salt ponds may be seen. These are prime candidates for real estate reclamation, and offer the last major opportunity to enlarge and restore the bay. A national wildlife refuge has been established. Palo Alto has already established a marsh nature interpretation center just off Highway 101. An inland area in Palo Alto is also worth a visit. Page Mill Road off State 82 bisects an industrial park and then winds through progressively steeper hill country, which appears destined for subdivisions into view lots. However, a study commissioned by the city, *Open Space Vs. Development,* prepared by the planning firm of Livingston and Blaney and available from the city of Palo Alto found that public costs of developing this area, parts of which are geologically unstable and fire-prone, would exceed any return in revenue. As a result, the city authorities decided to regulate and acquire land in the area to keep it open space. The report has become popular reading in other coastal communities besieged by proposals to subdivide what remains of the undeveloped coast. At South Laguna in southern California, an environmentally oriented plan generated by a volunteer group of planners, landscape architects and a geologist has received considerable community support. (For more information, contact Fred Lang, Lang & Wood, in South Laguna.)

Often scenic urban headlands are preempted for military purposes rooted in nineteenth-century doctrines of coastal defense. An example is the handsome headlands that flank the Golden Gate; however, the new GOLDEN GATE NATIONAL RECREATION AREA will incorporate a part of these.

AUDUBON CANYON RANCH, just fifteen miles north of Golden Gate Bridge, is an impressive blend of redwood forest with tidelands and nesting egrets. Turn onto State Highway One after crossing the bridge and continue to the ranch sign just north of Stimson Beach. A fund-raising drive spearheaded by local Audubon Society members saved this canyon from subdivision. It serves as a regional nature interpretation center, particularly for school classes. A milking barn has been transformed into a museum of the natural history of neighboring BOLINAS LAGOON. Nature trails have been kept to a minimum to protect the egret and heron rookeries in the redwood trees. An overview site permits observation of the nesting birds. Bolinas Lagoon, where they feed, has been spared the pressures of dredging and fill but not the threat of a freeway. The presence of the San Andreas fault argues for a restrained approach to development. (For more information, see "White Birds and Redwoods" by Harold Gilliam in *Audubon* for May 1972).

About forty miles north of San Francisco on State Highway One is BODEGA HEAD, a peninsula two and a half miles long. Plans to build a nuclear plant here were abandoned after a late revelation that the site lay astride an active earthquake fault, reaffirming the objections of environmentalists to the project. A large hole that marks the abandoned site is now filled with water, and is used by scuba divers to test their equipment. The University of California at Berkeley operates a marine field station here. Farther to the north, at Jenner, is the mouth of the RUSSIAN RIVER, where plans for the massive extraction of sand and gravel were defeated by an alliance of environmentalists and marine scientists, thus staving off yet another industrial intrusion.

About 170 miles north of San Francisco on State Highway One lies delightful MENDOCINO, a remote mill town that has become a noted art colony. Protective zoning conserves the community's legacy of Victorian architecture from being exploited by Destination Tourism. A windswept headland meadow is being preserved in its natural condition by the State of California. Nearby are three state parks with camping facilities: VAN DAMME, RUSSIAN GULCH and MACKERRICHER.

At Eureka, northern California's largest city, FORT HUMBOLDT STATE HISTORICAL MUSEUM has excellent exhibits on the days of redwood lumbering. Here can be observed the mouth of the EEL RIVER. Continuing siltation in the river basin from hydraulic gold mining and coastal logging has produced a rapid rate of erosion—four to eight inches a century, which is thirteen times the national average. Every ten years, over 310 million tons of rock and soil are carried away by the process.

REDWOOD NATIONAL PARK, located along Highway 101 in northern California between Orick and Crescent City, was authorized by Congress in 1968. The park is forty-six miles long and seven miles across at its greatest width. Three long-established state parks have been absorbed within its boundaries. (Early concern for preserving the coastal redwoods led to the formation of the California State Park System. The first park in the system, established in 1901 after an extensive campaign by the Sempervirens Club of San Jose, set aside the Big Basin redwood grove north of Santa Cruz. Through extensive fund-raising and private donations, the Save-the-Redwoods League, organized in 1918, saved many redwood groves that visitors now enjoy.) Since acquisition of many prime "in-holdings" is still in progress, visitors should not be surprised by No Trespassing signs and limited facilities. Park information centers are located in Crescent City and Orick. Aside from some heavy-handed industry propaganda on alleged dangers of "overripe" redwood stands, the MILLER-RELLIM DEMONSTRATION FOREST, located off Highway 101 directly south of Crescent City, offers a well-labeled nature trail walk as well as a concise plant and tree guide. Park trails lead to the shore, where seals, tidepools and rugged scenery abound. Swimming and surfing are dangerous owing to heavy undertow, jagged rocky shoals and cold waters. DRY LAGOON BEACH STATE PARK and BIG LAGOON COUNTY PARK, within a half-hour's drive of the park's south boundary along Highway 101, offer warm-water swimming in coastal lagoons and trout fishing in fresh water.

At CRESCENT CITY, approximately twenty miles from the Oregon border, a tetrapod, the masssive concrete form used to armor harbor breakwater structures, marks the entrance to the highway at the south end of the city. This twenty-five-ton form was carried inland by the 1964 seismic sea wave that inundated part of the community and resulted in the downtown community renewal project. The bay shore is used primarily as an open safety zone. The extensive logging debris on the shore is great for driftwood collectors and montage-builders; however, the same debris becomes a battering ram on the shoulders of a seismic sea wave. It is so extensive on the northern California coast, according to Dr. John Mero, an authority on coastal and marine mining, as to discourage shoreline mining for such things as gold and construction aggregate, since the debris would be hard to remove and might return on storm waves to destroy mining equipment.

Oregon

The Oregon coast, in sharp contrast to much of California, has many parks (of the green and open variety) and is far less congested. However, the many coastal campgrounds attract park-short Californians. FILLED TO CAPACITY signs may be encountered during the summer.

Oregon State University's MARINE SCIENCE CENTER at Newport, situated along Yaquina Bay on the central coast, contains an aquarium-museum that is open daily to the public. Live exhibits of native marine life include octopus, crabs and wolf eels. Visitors may pick up and inspect seastars, sea urchins, sea cucumbers and crabs in an intertidal handling pool. Displays also cover coastal geology, historic voyages and estuarine ecology. Books on marine science and natural history are available at the reception desk. Adjacent to the center is a marine research reserve for field studies on estuarine organisms and beach processes. Also located on the center grounds is the Oregon State Fish Commission Laboratory. The Fish Commission's *A Guide to Oregon's Rocky Intertidal Areas* (Educational Bulletin #5) describes thirty-three intertidal areas along the coast and identifies the most obvious species for beachcombers.

Nine miles north of Newport are the beautiful marine gardens at OTTER ROCK. Turn off Highway 101 towards Devil's Punch Bowl State Park and turn right on the last dead-end road before reaching the park. From the dead-end road, a good trail leads to the beach. Channels along the shore break up sandstone shelves into tidepool pockets colonized by purple sea urchins. Kelp beds rim the sea cliffs. Mussels and seastars flourish. The scenic promontory of CAPE FOULWEATHER was discovered by Captain James Cook on March 7, 1778—his first sight of the Pacific Northwest.

AGATE BEACH, just three miles north of Newport, attracts visitors in search of jasper, tiger eye, sard, fortification agate, bloodstones and other beach agates. The hunting is best during winter or spring when tides uncover great beds of gravel, with concentrations of stones washed out of the bank.

Along Coast Street, Newport's main oceanfront road, one may see evidence of bluff erosion that threatens the road as well as the houses along it.

One of the Pacific coast's more spectacular sights lies twenty-two miles south of Newport on Highway 101, where CAPE PERPETUA rises dramatically from the Pacific shore, literally thumbing its nose at the pounding breakers below. The cape, part of SIUSLAW NATIONAL FOREST, accommodates a U. S. Forest Service visitor information center with nature exhibits and movies. Trails that wind past Sitka spruce, Douglas fir, huckleberry and cascara, the tree with the laxative bark, lead to the intertidal area. Here one can see sponges, colonial ascidians and encrusting algae. Watch out for an incoming surf that rockets driftwood about. Visits at low tide are more revealing as well as safer than at high tide.

SEA LION CAVES, eleven miles north of Florence and thirty-nine miles south of Newport, is reputed by the U. S. National Forest Service to be the only mainland sea lion rookery in the world. Bounded by the Pacific and by Siuslaw National Forest, the cave is run as a commercial enterprise. An elevator brings visitors down to sea level. Sea birds—guillemots, puffins, cormorants and gulls—may also be observed.

The Oregon dunes stretch fifty miles along the coast between Florence and the Coos Bay area. The OREGON DUNES NATIONAL RECREATION AREA, established in 1972, is readily accessible from Highway 101. The dunes are constantly on the move,

blocking off creek mouths to form lakes, sandblasting fir forests, burying roads and encircling private residences. The eroding sandstone bedrock of the coast continually nourishes the wind-driven dunes. Watch for Japanese glass fishing floats among the flotsam along the shore. Watch out also for quicksand, broken glass and nails. "Current tetanus injections are a good idea but care in foot travel is a better one," notes the Forest Service. Winds can erase footprints, usher in fog, shut out visibility and create a bad scene for children who wander too freely, particularly where forest undergrowth is dense.

South of the dunes lies COOS BAY, a drowned rivermouth which extends inland about thirty miles. The bay provides an instructive glimpse into conflicts between natural marine features and urban demands, Oregon style. The inflow of nutrients from the bay drainage area and tidal mixing produce a rich food base. Dungeness crabs landed commercially at Coos Bay bring in a million dollars annually, after processing. Striped bass, salmon and cutthroat trout pass through the estuary, where flounder, sole and sand dabs pursue a more sedentary career. Upwards of 250 bird species—resident and migratory—frequent a state waterfowl refuge in PONY SLOUGH. Harbor seals may be viewed on spoil islands in the lower bay.

The economy of the area is dominated by lumber, whose uncontrolled side effects are cruelly evident. In the watershed area, huge clear cuts, poorly designed lumber roads and slash burning loosen the soil, and the resulting siltation of the bay buries shellfish and raises dredging costs. Clear cuts also expose once shady streams to warmer temperatures, upsetting the life cycle of trout and salmon. More enlightened lumber practices—such as leaving streamside buffer strips to maintain shade and screening effects, as well as prompt reseeding of cutover lands—are not so evident.

Pulp mill discharges of sulfite liquor and pulp debris can subvert the bay's natural richness. Dikes containing spent liquor often leak into the bay. A 1970 study by the University of Oregon's Institute of Marine Biology found that fifty acres of tidelands within one lumber company's plume and dispersion zone of discharge were barren of life. Because of poor water quality, the Oregon State Board of Health regards most of the bay as unsuitable for commercial clamming. (The major oyster-producing area—SOUTH SLOUGH in Charleston—still remained in healthy condition *at the time of this writing.*)

Extensive log storage areas may be viewed in the COOS RIVER, at ISTHMUS SLOUGH (alongside Highway 101 to the south of the city of Coos Bay) and at COALBEND SLOUGH. Bark and wood debris from such storage areas decompose and strip the water of oxygen. The shore itself is often layered with this debris, producing a substrate that is no substitute for mudflats. The bumping and pounding of logs with the tides squeeze marine plants out of existence. To reduce such carnage, lumber companies are beginning to store logs on land.

In 1970 the U. S. Army Corps of Engineers spent $750,000 to remove silt from bay navigation channels. The spoil is often dumped on bay wetlands to create airports and industrial land. A visit to SIMPSON PARK in North Bend gives a vivid insight into this practice. As adjacent wetlands are converted into a log-covered earthfill, the process has destroyed marine life, cheapened the park investment and usurped public access to the bayfront. The reward for this three-pronged attack is that the reclaimed lands are now worth about $1.2 million.

Civic awareness of such self-defeating development was sparked after students at the Oregon Institute of Biology made an ecological survey of the bay under the direction of the Institute's head, Paul Rudy. A subsequent report by the Department of the Interior recommended management steps to restore and protect the values of the bay. Some restrictions on harmful lumbering and dredging practices are now being implemented. (For more information, see *Management of Coos Bay, Oregon,* available from the Portland office of the Department of the Interior, Box 3621, Portland, Oregon 97208. The report contains a series of maps showing natural features as well as sources of contamination.) The city of COOS BAY has also embarked on a downtown renewal project which will relocate utilities underground, open a pedestrian mall and park, and add landscaping. Such renewal efforts are needed in waterfront cities that have deteriorated with age. VALLEJO in the San Francisco Bay area has reopened a derelict section of waterfront for use as a scenic public park.

A triad of state coastal parks can be reached by traveling fifteen miles west from Coos Bay on the Empire–Charleston highway. The first, SUNSET BAY, is a landlocked bay sheltered from the wind by a rim of sandstone bluffs. SHORE ACRES, in the middle, preserves the garden estate of a lumber magnate. The bluffs offer a good view of pounding winter waves. CAPE ARGO, at the end of the road, embraces three cove beaches. Bedrock shelves and cliffs rise from the sand to shelter tidepool communities. Offshore, the bark of sea lions can be heard. You may also stumble across huge mats of wood and bark fibers several feet thick that have drifted out of the bay and onto the ocean front.

In the salmon-canning city of ASTORIA, at the northern end of the Oregon coast, the COLUMBIA RIVER MARITIME MUSEUM contains shipping and fishing exhibits. Nearby is the reconstructed FORT CLATSOP NATIONAL MEMORIAL, where Lewis and Clark wintered in 1805–1806.

Washington

Although not as rich in parks as Oregon, the Washington coast offers the visitor two extraordinary views of the natural shore. In the state's southwest corner, LONG BEACH PENINSULA protects WILLIPA BAY, "probably the least affected by man's adverse industrial and agricultural activities of all the major bays on the west coast of the United States," according to the Department of the Interior's *National Estuary Study.* Highway 101 leads into the south end of the peninsula. Roads flank both sides, but public access to the bayfront is limited.

The bay's tidal range is extensive, with 32,000 of its 70,400 acres exposed at mean low water. Lush beds of eelgrass nourish waterfowl, including black brant, and shelter sticky herring egg masses. About 210 bird species, both resident and migrant, feast on the juicy mudflats or nest in the marshes. Oyster beds may be observed here at low tide. The beds are mainly in private ownership and harvesting by the public is frowned upon. Fresh oysters and littleneck clams may be procured at the cannery hamlets of NAHCOTTA and OYSTERVILLE.

Salmon, steelhead trout and shad cross the bay en route to spawning grounds in its eight tributary streams. Green sturgeon lurk in deeper waters, rising onto the flats to feed during high tide. Young flounder use the bay as a nursery. Dungeness crabs also flourish here. Harbor seals haul up at GRASSY ISLAND, on the bay side of Leadbetter Point. Beaver, muskrat and mink tracks may be found in the wetlands. A high water table on the peninsula nourishes trout-rich lakes and cranberry bogs.

While the Interior Department urges protection of this relatively unsullied bay, another government agency, the Pacific Soil and Water Conservation District, promotes reclamation of 6600 acres for pasture and silage. Careless lumber practices in the watershed provide siltloads that tend to hasten reclamation. The Army Corps of Engineers, which must dredge up the silt from navigation channels, has been happy to donate the spoil to this purpose. Draining and filling of lowlands for lagoon-type housing projects may also be seen.

FORT CANBY STATE PARK, at the peninsula's southern tip, provides physical and visual access to the mouth of the Columbia River as well as to Cape Disappointment and an ocean shore layered with lumber debris. On the exposed western slope, the floral cover is low and wind-pruned, whereas the protected eastern slope is densely covered with trees. The ocean surf that smashes into the bar-trapped mouth of the Columbia can leap twenty feet into the air. Such is the danger of the entrance that it has claimed two thousand vessels and fifteen hundred lives. At LEADBETTER POINT STATE PARK, occupying the northern tip of the peninsula, the terrain is much more gentle, embracing sand dunes, forest, a bay marsh and an ocean beach. For more information on this fascinating corner of Washington, see *Coast Country* by Lucile McDonald (Portland, Oregon: Binfords & Mort, 1966).

The rugged northern coast of Washington contrasts sharply with low-lying Long Beach Penin-

sula. Here the fabled rain forest of the OLYMPIC NATIONAL PARK and nearby CAPE FLATTERY thrive with a minimum of roadway. To see much of this region's ocean beaches, one must go on foot at low tide.

Along the southern portion of the park's ocean strip, between Queets and Ruby Beach, Highway 101 follows the shore. Between Ruby Beach and the park's northern boundary, CAPE ALAVA, a distance of approximately forty miles, only one road gives access—at La Push, a salmon harbor in the QUILLAYUTE INDIAN RESERVATION. Hiking along this roadless shore, one may see the maritime cedars that Indians hewed into dugout canoes, and which are now used for rowing shells. Black-tailed deer may visit the shore in early morning. The numerous creeks, some glacier-fed, are generally fordable in the summer. Don't feel dejected if the sun doesn't always shine. The shore is most dramatic—and most natural—as it wavers between billowing fog, shafted sunlight, sea squalls, and moonlit nights. Multicolored tidepools are strung along the shore like rough-hewn jewels. Rock islets may shelter eagle nests. Two excellent guides are available: *Trail Country* by Robert Wood (Seattle: Olympic Park Association, 1968) and *The Olympic Seashore* by Ruth Kirk (Olympic Natural History Association).

That this shore is unpaved is no accident. Lumber companies, resort operators and high-density recreation enthusiasts have been trying to properly civilize this dismayingly "primitive" and "undeveloped" strip for over half a century. Well-organized citizen and conservation groups, particularly from the Seattle area, appear forever prepared to mount protest marches in the face of the latest stratagem for "improvement." Tragically enough, national park officials sometimes feel compelled to promote conversion of the shore to a transportation right of way. Colliding with a demonstration in favor of road-building, Supreme Court Justice William Douglas, a long-time conservationist, wondered aloud, "Do roads have to go everywhere?"

The park does not extend into CAPE FLATTERY but ends at Cape Alava, the westernmost point of the coterminous United States. Much of the former is within a reservation occupied by the Makah Indians, the gray whale hunters of yore. The area covers about 16,000 acres, including twenty miles of ocean front. Cedar, hemlock and fir crown the coastal cliffs. Some unimproved roads struggle towards the cape's tip, but one must be prepared to walk part of the way. On the headland, sure enough, the usual military facility is to be seen in the form of Air Force hardware. The greatest threat to the cape's security and serenity appears to be from Alaskan oil tankers that invade the narrow Strait of Juan de Fuca. The thought of getting out the National Guard or thousands of volunteers to launder an oil-smeared cape poses an interesting logistical problem, causing one to wonder whether this section of the Pacific shore will eventually become a hostage to oil operations.

Cape Flattery would make a superb addition to Olympic National Park. However, the complications of ownership, tribal rights and acquisition costs have frustrated efforts in this direction.

Like the San Francisco Bay area, the PUGET SOUND REGION contains museums and exhibit centers devoted to its fascinating natural and social history. The PORT ANGELES PIONEER MEMORIAL MUSEUM at Port Angeles is one example. Others include the STATE HISTORY MUSEUM at Tacoma and the PACIFIC SCIENCE CENTER at Seattle. Institutions of higher learning such as the University of Washington in Seattle often have exhibits devoted to marine history. The LUMMI INDIAN RESERVATION, nationally recognized for its cultivation of salmon and oysters, is located north of Bellingham—an area that is also home for ARCO's large new refinery, built to receive Alaskan oil shipments. A ferry ride away from Seattle is scenic VICTORIA at the southern tip of Vancouver Island in British Columbia. On the way are the lovely SAN JUAN ISLANDS, also accessible by ferries. Worthwhile stops include the MARITIME MUSEUM, the FOREST SERVICE MUSEUM and THUNDERBIRD PARK, which contains totem poles and an Indian lodge.

Primary Sources

Natural History

BAILEY, HARRY. *The Climate of Southern California.* Berkeley: University of California Press, 1966.

BASCOM, WILLARD. *Waves and Beaches.* Garden City, New York: Anchor Books, 1964.

DURRENBERGER, ROBERT. *Elements of California Geography.* Palo Alto: National Press Books, 1968.

EMERY, K. O. *The Sea off Southern California.* New York: Wiley, 1960.

HEDGPETH, JOEL. *Introduction to Seashore Life of the San Francisco Bay Region and the Coast of Northern California.* Berkeley: University of California Press, 1962.

JAEGER, EDMUND, AND ARTHUR SMITH. *Introduction to the Natural History of Southern California.* Berkeley: University of California Press, 1966.

PEATTIE, RODERICK, ED. *The Pacific Coast Ranges.* New York: Vanguard, 1947.

RICKETTS, EDWARD, AND JACK CALVIN. *Between Pacific Tides.* Stanford: Stanford University Press, 1939; 4th ed., with extensive revisions by Joel Hedgpeth, 1968.

U. S. BUREAU OF SPORT FISHERIES AND WILDLIFE. *Proceedings of the 1970 Northwest Estuarine and Coastal Zone Symposium.* Portland: U. S. Department of the Interior, Bureau of Sport Fisheries and Wildlife, 1971.

U. S. DEPARTMENT OF THE INTERIOR. *National Estuary Study* (7 vols.). Washington: Superintendent of Documents, 1970.

U. S. OFFICE OF EMERGENCY PREPAREDNESS. *Geologic Hazards and Public Problems* (proceedings of a 1969 conference in San Francisco). Washington: Superintendent of Documents, 1970.

Indians

ANDERSON, EUGENE, JR. *The Chumash Indians of Southern California.* Banning, California: Malki Museum Press, 1968.

BROWNE, J. ROSS. "The Indians of California," in *Crusoe's Island.* New York: Harper & Bros., 1864.

BRYAN, BRUCE. *Archaeological Explorations of San Nicolas Island.* Los Angeles: Southwest Museum, 1970.

COLSON, ELIZABETH. *The Makah Indians.* Minneapolis: University of Minnesota Press, 1953.

DANIELS, ROGER, AND SPENCER OLIN. *Racism in California.* New York: Macmillan, 1970.

DRUCKER, PHILIP. *Cultures of the North Pacific Coast.* San Francisco: Chandler, 1965.

GUNTHER, ERNA. *Art in the Life of the Northwest Coast Indians.* Portland, Oregon: Portland Art Museum, 1966.

HEIZER, ROBERT, AND JOHN MILLS, EDS. *The Four Ages of Tsurai.* Berkeley: University of California Press, 1952.

HEIZER, ROBERT, AND M. A. WHIPPLE, EDS. *The California Indians: A Source Book.* Berkeley: University of California Press, 1951.

HOLM, BILL. *Northwest Coast Indian Art.* Seattle: University of Washington Press, 1965.

KROEBER, A. L. *Handbook of the Indians of California.* Bulletin of the Bureau of American Ethnology, 1925.

KROEBER, THEODORA. *The Inland Whale.* Berkeley: University of California Press, 1959.

LANDBERG, LEIF. *The Chumash Indians of Southern California.* Los Angeles: Southwest Museum, 1965.

MCFEAT, TOM, ED. *Indians of the North Pacific Coast.* Seattle: University of Washington Press, 1966.

MERRIAM, C. HART. *Ethnographic Notes on California Indian Tribes.* Berkeley: University of California Archaeological Research Facility Reports, 1966.

MOZINO, JOSÉ. *Noticias de Nutka,* translated and edited by Iris Higbie Wilson. Seattle: University of Washington Press, 1970.

ORR, PHIL. *Prehistory of Santa Rosa Island.* Santa Barbara: Santa Barbara Museum of Natural History, 1968.

ROGERS, DAVID. *Prehistoric Man of the Santa Barbara Coast.* Santa Barbara: Santa Barbara Museum of Natural History, 1929.

STERN, BERNHARD. *The Lummi Indians of Northwest Washington.* New York: AMS Press, 1969.

WATERMAN, T. T. *The Whaling Equipment of the Makah Indians.* Seattle: University of Washington Press, 1967.

Early Visitors

CAUGHEY, JOHN AND LAREE. *California Heritage.* Los Angeles: Ward Ritchie Press, 1962.

CHASE, DON. *Jedediah Strong Smith: He Opened the West.* Published by the author, Sebastopol, California.

CUTRIGHT, PAUL. *Lewis and Clark: Pioneering Naturalists.* Urbana: University of Illinois Press, 1969.

CUTTER, DONALD, ED. *The California Coast.* Norman: University of Oklahoma Press, 1969.

HAKLUYT, RICHARD. *Hakluyt's Voyages.* New York: Viking, 1965.

LEWIS, MERIWETHER. *Expedition of Lewis and Clark,* vol. 2. Ann Arbor: University Microfilms, 1966.

MARSHALL, JAMES AND CARRIE. *Vancouver's Voyage.* Vancouver: Mitchell Press, 1967.

MATHES, W. MICHAEL. *Vizcaino and Spanish Expansion in the Pacific Ocean.* San Francisco: California Historical Society, 1968.

RICKMAN, JOHN. *Journal of Captain Cook's Last Voyage to the Pacific Ocean.* Ann Arbor: University Microfilms, 1966.

TYLER, DAVID. *The Wilkes Expedition.* Philadelphia: The American Philosophical Society, 1968.

VANCOUVER, GEORGE. *Voyage and Discovery to the North Pacific Ocean and Round the World* (3 vols.). New York: Da Capo Press, 1967.

Exploitation and Conservation

CALIFORNIA DEPT. OF FISH AND GAME. *California's Living Marine Resources and Their Utilization.* Sacramento: California State Printing Office, 1971.

CALIFORNIA DEPT. OF NATURAL RESOURCES. *California Government and Forestry* (vol. 1). Sacramento: California State Printing Office, 1959.

CALIFORNIA DEPT. OF PARKS AND RECREATION. *California Coastline Preservation and Recreation Plan.* Sacramento: California State Printing Office, 1971.

CALIFORNIA RESOURCES AGENCY. *Landslides and Subsidence Geological Hazards Conference.* Sacramento: California State Printing Office, 1966.

CAUGHEY, JOHN. *History of the Pacific Coast of North America.* New York: Prentice-Hall, 1938.

CITY OF SANTA BARBARA. *Report of Activities of the Environmental Quality Advisory Board.* 1971, 1972.

DODDS, GORDON. *The Salmon King of Oregon.* Chapel Hill, North Carolina: University of North Carolina Press, 1963.

DUMKE, G. S. *The Boom of the Eighties in Southern California.* San Marino: Huntington Library, 1944.

FREY, HERBERT, RONALD HEIN, AND JACK SPRUILL. *The Natural Resources of Upper Newport Bay.* California Dept. of Fish and Game, 1970.

GARDNER, BARBARA, ED. *The Crowded Coast* (proceedings of a conference on California coastal zone management). Los Angeles: University of Southern California Center for Urban Affairs, 1971.

INMAN, DOUGLAS, AND BIRCHARD BRUSH. "The Coastal Challenge," *Science,* July 6, 1973.

MARX, WESLEY. *The Frail Ocean.* New York: Coward-McCann, 1967; Ballantine, 1969.

———. *Oilspill.* New York: Sierra Club, 1971.

———. "The Fall and Rise of Sewage Salvage," *Bulletin of the Atomic Scientists,* May 1971.

McDONALD, LUCILE. *Coast Country.* Portland, Oregon: Binfords & Mort, 1966.

McKEON, STEVE. "Beach Access," *Stanford Law Review,* February 1970.

McWILLIAMS, CAREY. *Southern California Country.* New York: Duell, Sloan and Pearce, 1946.

OGDEN, ADELE. *The California Sea Otter Trade, 1784–1848.* Berkeley: University of California Press, 1941.

ORANGE COUNTY PLANNING DEPT. *The Physical Environment of Orange County.* Santa Ana, California, 1971.

SANDERS, NORMAN. "Port Hueneme, California—A Study in Coastal Anthropo-geomorphology," in *Yearbook,* Association of Pacific Coast Geographers, 1966.

SAN FRANCISCO BAY CONSERVATION AND DEVELOPMENT COMMISSION. *San Francisco Bay Plan Supplement.* Sacramento: California State Printing Office, 1968.

SCAMMON, CHARLES. *The Marine Mammals of the North-Western Coast of North America.* San Francisco: Carmany, 1874. (See also an article on Scammon by Wesley Marx in *American Heritage,* June 1969.)

U. S. BUREAU OF SPORT FISHERIES AND WILDLIFE. *Proceedings of the 1970 Northwest Estuarine & Coastal Zone Symposium.* Washington, 1971.

U. S. DEPARTMENT OF THE INTERIOR. *National Estuary Study* (7 vols.). Washington: Superintendent of Documents, 1970.

U. S. OFFICE OF EMERGENCY PREPAREDNESS. *Geologic Hazards and Public Problems* (proceedings of a 1969 conference in San Francisco). Washington: Superintendent of Documents, 1970.

WILSON, BASIL, AND ALF TORUM. *The Tsunami of the 1964 Alaskan Earthquake.* Washington: U. S. Army Coastal Engineering Research Center, 1968.

WINTER, OSCAR OSBURN. *The Great Northwest.* New York: Knopf, 1966.

Literature

BENNETT, MELBA. *The Stone Mason of Tor House.* Los Angeles: Ward Ritchie Press, 1966.

BROWNE, J. ROSS. *The Coast Rangers.* Balboa Island, California: Paisano Press, 1959.

CAUGHEY, JOHN AND LAREE. *California Heritage.* Los Angeles: Ward Ritchie Press, 1962.

COVERDALE, JOAN. *I Share This Marsh.* Seal Beach, California: Whale and Eagle Publishers, 1973.

DANA, RICHARD. *Two Years Before the Mast.* Boston: Houghton Mifflin, 1911.

DILLON, RICHARD. *J. Ross Browne.* Norman: University of Oklahoma Press, 1965.

ERICKSON, URSULA, AND ROBERT PEARSALL. *The Californians: Writings of Their Past and Present* (2 vols.). San Francisco: Hesperian House, 1961.

GREELEY, HORACE. *An Overland Journey.* New York: Knopf, 1964.

HEDGPETH, JOEL. "Philosophy on Cannery Row," in *Steinbeck: The Man and His Work.* Corvallis: Oregon State University Press, 1971.

HOLBROOK, STEWART. *Holy Old Mackinaw.* New York: Macmillan, 1938; Ballantine, 1971.

JEFFERS, ROBINSON. *The Selected Poetry of Robinson Jeffers.* New York: Random House, 1959.

LAMBERT, GAVIN. *The Slide Area.* New York: Dial, 1968.

LUCIA, ELLIS. *The Land Around Us: A Treasury of Pacific Northwest Writing.* Garden City, N. Y.: Doubleday, 1969.

MELTZER, DAVID, ED. *San Francisco Poets.* New York: Ballantine, 1971.

MILLER, HENRY. *Big Sur and the Good Life.* New York: New Directions, 1957.

MILLER, MAX. *I Cover the Waterfront.* New York: Dutton, 1931.

MUIR, JOHN. *Steep Trails.* Boston: Houghton Mifflin, 1918.

POWELL, LAWRENCE. *California Classics.* Los Angeles: Ward Ritchie Press, 1971.

STEINBECK, JOHN. *The Log from the Sea of Cortez.* New York: Viking, 1951.

STEVENSON, ROBERT LOUIS. *The Silverado Squatters.* London: Chatto & Windus, 1883.

Index

Figures in **bold type** refer to photographs.